How To Improve Your Charisma

Stop Social Anxiety, Build Magnetic Self-Esteem & Learn The Science To Talk To Anyone With Effective Social Communication, Emotional Intelligence & Public Speaking Skills

Author: Mark Page

Introduction

What is Charisma?

Charisma is the ability of a person to attract, captivate, and impact the people that are around him/her. Most times, it is easy to note a person who has charisma; other times, it is not. To categorically say the skills or the qualities of a charismatic person can be a bit hard when it comes to comparing them with other people who are less charismatic. In this sense, it becomes difficult to say what those who are not charismatic lack.

There are some lucky individuals who possess a great amount of what is called "charismatic potential", and they are able to quickly learn from other people by observing their charming behavior, positive body language, voice inflection, and emotional display. They are chameleon-like in a sense; charisma is an unspoken language, and these fortunate folks are able to pick up that language by the time they reach early adulthood, usually.

For the rest of us, it's important to remember that charisma is, by nature, a learned set of skills. There is no gate barring us from entering this world of success and popularity. We simply have to follow in the naturally charismatic person's footsteps, and do what they do, see what they see.

To further define charisma, it becomes a bit more complicated because there are different categories of charismatic people. Some categories of charismatic people are usually calm and depend on their charms, rather than their words to influence people. Another type of charismatic people are those who are excellent and passionate communicators. With the kind of enthusiasm they display when they are talking, it is easy for them to sweep people off their feet.

Making the decision to learn to become more charismatic is in investment in your life—if you're ready to be more successful, more well-liked, and happier and more comfortable with yourself, then get ready for some positive change!

Generally, charisma can be said to be a product of excellent communication as well as interpersonal skills. This points us to the fact that a person can easily boost his or her charisma if they want to. People usually make the mistake of thinking that charisma is something a person is born with. This isn't entirely true because it is an attribute that does not have to be innate. Charisma is learnable when you practice and with reinforcement over time.

Chapter 1.   What Is Charisma?

C harisma is that thing that special people have that's really hard to define with words but is something everyone can recognize when they see it in someone.

Someone who has charisma naturally draws in people and for some hard-to-define reason, appears to be leading the pack.

From someone on the outside, a person with charisma seems to project a certain amount of power outside their actual legal or political power.

If it's hard to define what charisma is exactly, then we can at least try to explain what the elements of charisma are.

What exactly makes a person charismatic? What is it about charismatic people that makes them natural leaders who command respect and inspire others?

Some people say charisma is about power, and some say it's about presence, the ability to empathize, projecting confidence, leadership, and many others.

Charismatic people seem to be so special that even among charismatic people, no two are alike, and the way they seem to project their charisma seems to be slightly different from each other.

But, there are a few common elements or "building blocks," so to speak, that many people with charisma share, and that's what we're going to talk about in this chapter.

In my opinion, the things that make a person charismatic include having a presence, having influence, and having the ability to empathize with others.

Of course, it doesn't always come in the same amount, and not every charismatic person has all of them.

Having A Presence

The first element that seems to be common among people with charisma is their presence. I'm not talking about just being present as simply being there. I'm talking about being present as in being one of the most, if not the most important person in the room.

They walk into a room full of people, and everyone seems to feel their energy spread around the room and wrapping everyone.

When they talk, everyone seems to want to listen, and when they start taking action, everyone seems to want to see what they're up to.

They're attention magnets that draw people in without looking like they're making any effort at all. They make their presence known and make it all look effortless.

At the same time, they just don't draw in attention, but they also seem to be able to pay attention to anyone and everyone.

When they're talking to you, you somehow feel like they're really there. They make you feel like what you're saying really matters, and they make you feel very important.

It seems as if being acknowledged by them is a very big thing and that they're passing on some of their powers to you because when a charismatic person gives you their attention, everyone else also seems to pay attention to you as well.

Having Influence

When charismatic people talk, everyone seems to be compelled to listen. When they give orders, people seem to just follow. When they express emotions, everyone else seems to feel the same emotions.

They seem to display a certain amount of power over people that make other people feel compelled to follow their lead.

Remember that religious event I went to with that charismatic leader? I'm almost sure that if he told those thousands of people in that event to strip naked right then and there, they probably would have.

There's something about the way charismatic people talk and carry themselves that make people feel convinced that they're following the right leader.

Charismatic people display a certain amount of strength that makes people believe that this person is someone who can do everything they say and more.

They also know how to stir people's emotions and inspire people to make changes in their lives or to take action about something.

Having Empathy

Empathy is having the ability to put yourself in someone else's shoes, and people with charisma have a lot of empathy.

They project a sense of warmth that people seem to feel comfortable around them, and they seem to be able to connect with anyone.

It's mostly because they know how to put themselves in someone else's situation and completely understand where they are coming from.

Because of this ability, they can easily determine how to communicate with other people effectively, using the particular techniques that will work with a particular person.

They understand what makes other people tick, and they know how to get people to feel comfortable with them because they are in tune with the other person's feelings.

Building Your Charisma

So now that we know what characteristics are present in charismatic people as well as the basic elements that makeup charisma itself, we can structure the rest of the book into giving you what you need in order to build your charisma.

Now before we proceed, I know that charisma seems to come naturally to some people, and you might believe the same thing.

While it's true that certain individuals seem to have charisma naturally, it doesn't mean that it's something that can't be built, developed, and improved.

Charisma can be learned, and if it can be learned, it can be taught. If it can be taught and learned, then it can be developed and improved.

Building Your Presence

The main ingredient of presence is having confidence. It's so big that I'm going to dedicate a whole chapter just in building and projecting your confidence, which should be the one after this.

Aside from building your confidence, you also have to start considering the kind of reputation you currently have.

Then, you have to analyze if it's something that helps give you credibility and the respect of other people or if it's something that you regret having, and that makes people lose respect for you.

If it's something that you think is good, then you can keep it and build your reputation further on top to develop a solid one that really impresses the people who hear of you.

If it's bad, then you have to do something to immediately turn it around and build yourself a new one from scratch.

Let's start the process by making you realize how important your reputation is and why you should work on it.

First, take these questions and answer them in your head:

1. What's the biggest mistake you regret ever making?
2. What's the single biggest embarrassing thing that's ever happened to you?

Now your answer to these two questions may be one and the same, or it might be different from each other.

Whichever the case, are they something that other people know and still remind you about?

If your answer is yes, then that thing has become somewhat a part of your reputation, and well, you can't build your charisma on that. It has to be either completely buried, given a twist, or written over.

Normally, a single event doesn't really define your reputation. I mean, it can if it's really big, but normally, your reputation is based on something that you often do or often happens to you.

For example, you can be known in college as that guy who can drink a lot and never get drunk, or you can be known as that guy who's really good a pickup lines.

But, the thing about your reputation is that if you do one big thing that's inconsistent with your reputation, you can break the whole thing.

For example, a politician who has a reputation for honesty and integrity usually builds it by having a record of good governance. However, if suddenly, that same politician is suddenly exposed as a sexual predator even by just one victim, then their good reputation will almost instantly disappear and become that of a sexual predator.

I know, reputations can be very fragile, and getting it ruined can be scary. But, I'm here hoping and assuming that you haven't sexually assaulted someone or did some heinous crime that could get exposed one day.

Anyway, your reputation is very important because it's one of those things that people use to judge you before they even meet you or get to know you.

If you've ever met your idol before then, you know the feeling. I once had the pleasure of talking to Aaron Rodgers in one celebrity golfing event. I'm not a Packers fan, but still, this man is known for being the top quarterback at the time. That was his reputation, and because of this reputation, I felt his presence when he stopped to talk to some fans at the event, and he had this presence because well, he's a great football player.

In my job, I also get to occasionally meet with politicians to discuss a few things that concern our company's impact on the public, and we participate in charities and fundraisers organized by these politicians, so I get to see them in action.

When I was new to the job, I sometimes forgot to do my research and don't know who these politicians are. I just see them and think they're some important person, but because I don't know who they are exactly, I don't feel their presence too much.

But, when I started really doing my research, everyone I met with a good reputation started to feel to me like they have this presence just because I heard about their accomplishments.

So, you have to take care of your reputation. Ideally, you would want to be known for something good and amazing.

Whatever it is that you decide to build a reputation on, you have to make sure to stick to it consistently as if it's marked on your forehead. You can't compromise because even that single time you compromised can tarnish your reputation.

Now in order to build your reputation, you have to do whatever you say you'll do. You can't go around telling people that you're planning to do this or that but never really follow through. If you do that, then you'll instead have a reputation of being someone who is all talk.

Another thing you should do is you should look the part. If you want to build your reputation, usually a good place to start is always to look clean and well-groomed.

You can't go around trying to build your reputation looking like a mess and smelling like you haven't showered in days.

If you have a bad reputation in the past, as I said, you have the choice of burying it, twisting it, or writing over it.

For example, if you were once known as that nerd back in high school, then you can either bury it by not talking about it and avoiding people who still remember it and talk about it.

You can also give it a twist, meaning you can use it as a starting point as if it was a stepping stone for you to get to where you are now.

If that sounds confusing, then as an example, let me give you all those before and after images you see on weightloss products. The people modeling would tell you how they used to weigh over three hundred pounds, but now they're fit.

What I mean is you can spin your story as that of a transformational one. People love transformational stories of how someone changed and improved themselves.

In writing over your reputation, you just completely disregard the bad reputation you once had, and you try to build a good reputation out of something else, which could make people ignore your previously bad reputation in favor of this new one you're building.

For example, if people knew you once as that kid who used to get in trouble all the time, then you can try to write over it by building a reputation for being a helpful person. You'll still be that kid who used to get in trouble all the time, but people will eventually know you for your helpfulness.

Whatever you decided to do, make sure always to be aware of and to take care of your reputation. It's really going to help you a lot when it comes to your presence.

Building Your Influence

Influencing others is a mix of having confidence and having great communication skills.

You can't influence someone if you can't communicate. At the same time, you won't be able to communicate effectively if you lack confidence.

Also, in order to influence people, you have to have conviction. It means that you really believe in whatever it is that you're trying to stand up for.

You can't really influence someone if they sense that you really don't believe in whatever it is that you're trying to sell them or make them believe.

You can fake your conviction and make people believe you, but eventually, you'll either get too exhausted of pretending, or you'll be exposed as a fraud, and people will stop listening to you.

You also have to be someone people can trust. People have to know that you're not going to lead them into something that could hurt them.

People have to be able to trust you on your word, that if you give them a promise or if you make deals with them, that you'll stick to your word and fulfill your end of the bargain.

That way, when you say something, people will always believe you, and they will always be ready to listen to you.

This reminds me of how I learned always to pay my debts ever since I was young. I didn't have good money skills back when I was a lot younger and always overspent. So, I was that guy who always had to borrow money.

I realized at an early age that people don't easily trust other people, especially when it comes to their money and possessions.

So, in order for people to trust me, I have to make sure to keep my word. If I borrow from someone, I always made sure they were paid on the day I said I'll pay them back.

I'm a lot better with money now and haven't had the need to borrow money in years now, but I know that I can always count on friends and family to lend me money when I need it because they know I'm good for it.

I remember losing my job once and needed to borrow money for rent, so I borrowed a thousand dollars from a friend, and he lent it to me without any questions because he knew I was going to pay him back.

So your trustworthiness is very important. People don't listen to people they don't trust, and if nobody listens to you, then you won't have any influence over anyone.

Another thing that builds trust is being personal, meaning putting yourself out there for people and risking vulnerability.

If you're always guarded and won't trust people, then you can't expect people to trust you either.

You have to open yourself up to people if you want them to trust you. You have to be willing to be vulnerable if you want people to really be open to you as well.

Building Empathy

When you know how to empathize, the people you interact with will start feeling like you're someone they can be comfortable with.

People are usually comfortable with people who they think understand them and those who they feel they have a connection with.

Strong bonds usually form between people who have shared experiences. This is the reason why we become friends with the people we have a lot in common with. It's also why we try to engage in group activities with our friends and valued family members.

We go on vacations, watch movies together, eat out - anything that we would enjoy with the people we value because the shared experience strengthens the bonds of the relationship.

Empathy is kind of like having these shared experiences, but instead of experiences, it's mostly about emotions.

When you empathize with someone, you try to see where they're coming from, and you try to adjust your interactions with them based on what you understand about them.

Now in order to build your empathy, the first thing you should do is to keep an open mind. You can't be close-minded, and you can't let your biases stop you from trying to understand other people.

Also, you have to really pay attention to the people you're interacting with, so you can really learn more about them.

You have to know to ask the right questions to give you an idea of what these other people are thinking and feeling, and you have to be careful not to pass judgment because that could close the dialogue.

Also, you have to learn to be quiet and observant of the other person. Instead of talking more, you have to listen more, and when you're listening, you have to really listen.

Don't get distracted, and don't interrupt when other people are still talking. You have to learn to keep quiet and let them talk, while at the same time, you also have to actively show them that you're listening by giving bits of feedback like nodding while they are talking.

You have to be concerned about what motivates people instead of simply focusing on what they actually did.

I know this might come off as being an extreme example, but try to imagine yourself working security at a department store, and you catch someone shoplifting.

Of course, shoplifting is illegal, and shoplifters have to be punished, but try to learn why the shoplifter did it.

If they were shoplifting medicine, then you might want to ask why out of everything they could steal at the store, they tried to steal medicine.

Maybe they'll tell you their loved one got sick and they're currently living in their car with no money even to buy some medicine.

You don't have to set the shoplifter free, but at least you get to understand where they're coming from, and you can treat them with just a little more respect than someone who casually steals a handbag or jewelry. Of course, this example is very rare if it happens at all.

Notes

Chapter 2.   Obstacles Many Of Us Face Regarding Charisma

Of course, if being charismatic were easy, everyone would do it. Let's talk about the obstacles many of us face regarding our charisma, learned or otherwise.

The Importance of Knowing Our Worth

This can be a very challenging task, and it's not necessarily our fault if we're out of touch with our own personal sense of value. Perhaps we were raised by a care-giver who put us down, or lived with a sibling who constantly berated us. Maybe we had a long-term relationship with a partner who was toxic, and who whittled away our self-esteem. Whatever the reason for your flagging self-worth, understand that a) it's not your fault and b) it is your responsibility to do something about it. Healing can take a lot of time, but that's no reason to ignore the need for it. The best time to start something new is today, and right now.

A frequent topic of debate is whether it's true that "we can do anything". For instance, not everyone's capable of becoming a prima ballerina or a professional quarterback. However, if we zero in on this statement, and add some detail to it, it's actually true, if:

- We make sure that our bodies are capable of the task, and discover if there's help to assist us.

- We take the time to do the work necessary to accomplish the "thing", and

- Make sure the thing is something we truly want to do.

You might not ever break into professional American football, but you could turn out to be an excellent football coach at your local Boys and Girls club, or even play in an amateur league. You might not ever perform the Nutcracker at Radio City Music Hall, but you can certainly perform in local events, strengthen your body, and achieve your dream of becoming a dancer. Even those without the use of their legs have ran in marathons, played basketball, or performed in dance concerts. The key elements here are *focus, will, and determination.*

Now let's focus on you. What have you achieved that is still a source of satisfaction and pride to this day? If you've not yet achieved anything you feel is worthy of respect, what would you *like* to achieve? Also, go back and look at things you might not consider achievements, but with a positive eye. Perhaps you're downplaying yourself and masking real, impressive accomplishments.

There are statements you need to make, right now, in order to better yourself and put yourself in the charismatic mindset.

These aren't promises—promises can be broken, especially if we're making them to ourselves. These are *statements*:

- I have the potential to achieve great things. I was born with this potential, and no one can take it away from me.

- I will not remain idle in my daily life. I will move forward and be a person of action.

- Following action, I will also give myself permission to rest, and relax. Both action and rest are necessary ingredients to success.

- I will not allow myself to pity myself. There's nothing to pity about me. I am okay.

- I will shift my focus from other people I used to think were better, to myself. I am good enough.

- I will dare to question myself, in order to make sure I'm authentic in my endeavors and behavior. Questioning does not mean hating. I refuse to engage in self-loathing.

- I am going to tap into my potential and achieve more with it.

Understand that you will never please everyone. If you believe that you can, you'll soon learn that trying to please everyone pleases no one, and ignores important care of yourself. Make peace with this and realize that not everyone is for everybody else. It's a wide world out there. You will find the people that you connect with.

Your opinions matter, and they also may change, and that is okay. Don't hide yourself for fear of being unpopular. At the same time, have the strength to *examine* your thoughts and opinions when you gain information and other people's points of view. It's okay to concede that you were wrong, or ignorant of something. Admitting that shows greatness, humility, and a mind that's not afraid to learn and grow.

Pleasing other people is not the point of the game. If it happens, great! If it doesn't, that's okay. Desperation is something that naturally drives others away from us; when we show this in our need to please others, we actually drive them away. When you're not afraid to displease or even offend others with your opinions, it shows strength and confidence. Don't *try* to offend, or take joy in offending others, because that's extremely unappealing, however, when you refuse to change what's vital and *true* about yourself to impress others, that in itself is incredibly impressive.

You will make the right connections with the right people when you stand up for yourself with both strength and integrity.

Integrity is the name of the game, and having integrity shows that you don't consider human interaction a game. Other people are just as important as you are; no one should ever be placed above or below someone else. When you are capable of empathy and can put yourself in another's shoes, your words and actions will maintain integrity, and other people will find it easier to relate to you, as well as have respect for you.

What happens when your values change, and you make choices or take action that you would never have in the past? You can still maintain integrity. Integrity simply means that you act and speak in accordance with what you believe, and beliefs change as we mature. Integrity can and should be maintained throughout our lives. Never let fear, your own ennui, or other people's threats coerce you into being corrupted.

Our Inner "Weather" And How It Effects Our Outer Presence

Getting back to our "presence", when we find ourselves in social situations, what's going on inside our heads at the time greatly effects how others perceive us. Later on in the book we'll discuss ways to cultivate happier mindsets and tackle charisma-killers such as anxiety, stress, and depression.

Right now, let's focus on the immediate need for a clear, calm mind to project the best presence and maintain optimum charisma.

The nervousness you feel inside will be readily visible on the outside. Just like genuine joy, awkwardness is also contagious.

Refuse to feel shame. If you've made a mistake, it's perfectly acceptable and natural to feel *regret* regarding making that mistake. Then, using our determination (if the mistake only effected us) or our empathy (if it effected someone else) we can strive to correct that mistake, or at least ensure that it never happens again. In social situations however, shame should be left at the door. It doesn't serve us, and has no place in the charismatic person's repertoire or vocabulary.

What happens when you say something that offends someone? For starters, do not immediately apologize. Stand your ground, not with arrogance, but with quiet strength. Listen to the other person and strive to learn what about your statement was offensive. See if you can learn anything from that person's point of view, and be thankfully vocal about it if you do. Make statements such as "I see where you're coming from." Then, if the emotions have cooled and you've made every effort to understand the other person, you may choose to offer an apology—but make sure you can do that with honesty.

Stop adding "I'm sorry" into every other moment of a conversation. It's neither genuine, nor attractive.

Lastly, if you haven't done this enough already, start practicing the art of thinking for yourself.

 Don't just go along with the crowd.

Examine the information you're given with an open mind, but don't be gullible. Become your own person.

Social Awkwardness Explained

When it comes to social awkwardness, there is a lot of *bad* advice out there. For starters, it doesn't matter if "everyone" has felt socially awkward at one point or another—that's not going to help you, not one bit. It also doesn't help to tell you to just "snap out of it" or imagine everyone in the room naked.

I mean, that would be even more awkward, right?

The art of social fluency takes practice. The most common reason people are socially awkward is because they are simply not in enough social situations to have acquired any practice or skills. If you want to be charismatic, you're going to have to do the work; there are no shortcuts.

Spending more time with people, you're going to begin to develop a sense of conversational and social rhythm: when to speak, and when to listen; when to tell a joke and when to keep the topic serious. If you spend most of your time alone, there's no way you're going to achieve this kind of intuitive interactional skill set. Watching actors in conversation might be a start, but we're also not always seeing characters at their best, and most importantly, *we* are not in the conversation—we're only watching it on the screen.

Anything you're skilled at—usually, unless you have a particular knack or gift in that certain area—you will have started out with some degree of awkwardness. Driving a car, writing a resume, mastering a video game, shaving, curling your hair—*it all takes patience and practice.* So resign yourself to the fact that if you want to be charismatic, you're going to need time, patience, and practice. Then approach this task with passion, because that will help too!

Muscle memory pertains to speaking, also. It also helps us with our facial expressions. We mimic each other all of the time, this is how babies learn to speak and express themselves, and this is how we learn to convey the emotions we feel—by watching other people.

The more you work those muscles in a certain way to connect with a certain idea or emotion, the easier it will be, the more *natural* it will become, to express yourself with ease and grace in the future.

Social awkwardness comes when we don't exercise these muscles often enough. Spending too much time by ourselves can make these skills "rusty", or underdeveloped.

Determining Whether You're on the AS (Autism Spectrum), and Why It's Not a Bad Thing If You Are

Everyone in fifty-nine people in the world will be born with autism. Male children are more apt to be on the autism spectrum than women. What is autism? For starters, it's not necessarily a setback. While approximately one third of people on the spectrum have some amount of intellectual disability and/or are non-verbal, others, such as those with Asperberg's Syndrome, do not. (Pronounced asz-*PURGER'S*). You see, autism is a *spectrum* of brain behavior and recognition. There are many different ways to be on the autism spectrum.

Asperger's is called a "high-functioning" placement of autism. One of the trademarks of having Asperger is having an acute interest bordering on obsession in a certain topic or topics. While this can be challenging during childhood (imagine an elementary school age kid trying to have in-depth discussions of World War II or cryptobiology and you'll get an idea), for adults, it can actually be quite an advantage.

A kid obsessed with dinosaurs to the point of memorizing every bone of every species uncovered could have quite a career at a museum or professor of paleontology.

A trait that occurs in people with Asperger's is also a large vocabulary obtained at a young age. People with Asperger's may discover that they intimidate people with their knowledge and vocabulary, but ironically feel intimidated themselves by those people.

What's important to realize is that very often, people with Asperger's don't realize they have a "problem", generally speaking, until adulthood, and their behaviors and the way they look at the world is only labelled a problem by other people, or by themselves if they've been shamed for being awkward in social situations. People on the autism spectrum simply process the information that life gives them differently. That does not make them necessarily "stupid" or "weird". They often have mental and imagination-based gifts that people not on the spectrum do not possess.

However, having Asperger's can pre-dispose you to:

- Avoidance of eye contact (without even realizing it!). A classic sign is someone with Asperger's telling a story to someone, but looking past their shoulder or away while telling it, often making the listener ask, "What are you looking at?"

- Difficulty taking turns.

- Difficulty in making new friends.

- Being prone to conversations that revolve around yourself and your own interests.

- Occasionally, socially-inappropriate behavior. This usually stems from processing things differently, and often out of an attempt to be humorous in a social setting.

- Taking things literally and not understanding common social cues, such as high-fiving, or expressions like "sharp as a whip" to indicate intelligence.

- Some Aspie folks have heightened senses, such as the sense of smell, making those who wear too much cologne or perfume unbearable to be around.

- Finally, for someone with Asperger's, it may be difficult to express their impressions about things to non-AS people. Many people with Asperger's also have something called "synesthesia", where they see music in shades of colors, or can describe the flavor of something in number patterns or unusual choice of words. For these people, senses become combined or switched around.

Since there is a lot more awareness about the autism spectrum now, kids diagnosed early enough get special help at school, such as small classes where they meet once a day to go through "typical" social situations and learn good choices and responses that will keep them in the loop. And while becoming inauthentic to one's self is never a good idea, even to gain popularity, we all have social "tics" and quirks that can be worked through to make us engage with other people more comfortably and smoothy. People with Asperger's just sometimes need a bit more help in that area.

If you think you might have Asperger's, talking to your doctor or therapist, or taking an online test can help you determine whether the description fits you. Once knowing this about yourself, it can be easier zeroing in on the social skills you need to work on the most.

Just remember, there is nothing shameful about being born on the autism spectrum. It's genetic, it's common, and people on the spectrum can live a full, vibrant, and fulfilling life.

If you are on the spectrum, or know that you have Asperger's, there are ways that you can get an edge on improving your social prowess. Begin by making a list of things that make you uncomfortable, socially. Separate them into these three categories:

- Things That Confuse Me (such as how to begin a conversation, tell a funny story)

- Things That Worry Me (such as the fact that you're not social enough, or what other people will think of you if you try to become more social)

- Excuses I Make To Avoid Being Social (such as taking on extra shifts at work, or binging an entire television series over a weekend)

Take a good, hard look at the things that worry you. If any of them sound silly, then that's a good thing! That means you're halfway towards eliminating them altogether. Underline or circle any of the worries that look less worrisome once you read them over.

Next, look at your excuses. Becoming more charismatic involves self-analyzing, and this is a challenging task for *everyone,* not just folks on the spectrum.

Which of these excuses can be lessened (such as only watching three episodes per weekend of a show), and which would you be able to tackle first, so that over time, you slowly eliminate all of them?

Face your social fears, but do it slowly, one step at a time. There is no need to push yourself here—just *wanting* to get better at socializing is a step in the right direction. As long as you make steady progress, you will reach your goal.

Pay attention to when you try something new that landed on your list of "Worries". What happened when you tried it? How did everyone react? Chances are, it will not have been as bad, or not have been bad at all, as you first feared. Picture how you would react if you met someone who say, stumbled in their words or made an awkward joke. Would you have empathy for them, or would you ridicule them? Once you see that most people will opt to be kind in a social setting, it will be easier for you to reduce your fears in a realistic way.

Finally, if you exhibit any physical symptoms in social settings (or when you're preparing to go to one), such as feelings of panic, trouble breathing, sweating, increased heart rate or dizziness, consider talking to your doctor about trying anxiety medication or CBD. CBD is a non-narcotic derivate of the cannabis plant.

It cannot make you feel "high" or intoxicated, but it has been proven to be an excellent tool in fighting anxiety and depression. Many people use it with good results, not just people with Asperger's.

Other steps to help in social settings include:

- Learning and understanding anything that's confusing to you. Reach out to a trusted family member or friend to discuss and even "practice" things that have baffled you in past social settings. Once you've tried a little in private, go out and see if you can gracefully get through these social cues in public, such as at a restaurant, at a library or store, on public transit, at a ball game.

- Learn the fine art of listening. Remember the tip to study the color of someone's eyes? This helps making eye contact comfortable for both the observer and the person being observed. When you listen to someone, give that person validation if they talk about their emotions. "When he raised his voice at me in front of everyone I felt so angry, and also ashamed." "Of course you did! I would, too." Ask the person questions to clarify anything they said.

- Keep your posture straight. If you need physical stimulation to stay focused, you can play with the straw of your drink or subtly tap one finger to your thumb at a time.

- If you're feeling overwhelmed, you can gracefully excuse yourself from the conversation by saying, "Excuse me for a moment. I'm enjoying talking with you, but I have to take care of something real quick." Remember to smile to leave them with a feeling of friendliness and warmth. They might reach out to shake your hand and say "Nice meeting you" or "It was a pleasure". Simply shake their hand, add a smile, and say "Same."

Finally, if you feel like having the support of a community would do you some good, seek out your local autism peer support group. There you can find others who are going through what you are, and who might have additional tips and tricks that have worked for them in social situations.

Notes

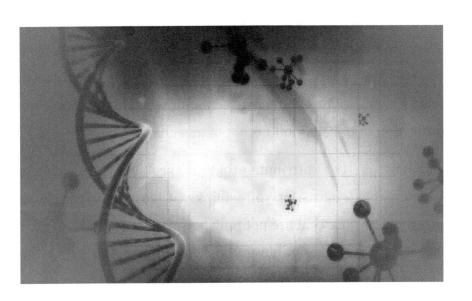

Chapter 3.   Elements of Charisma

R egardless of your situation and your aims as a person, one of the essential requirements for success in life is the charisma of an individual. This is the quality that will enable you to have full command of a room and also endear other people to you. This is what will also convince other people of the ideas you have. Every leader who has been able to win the love and admiration of devoted followers possess charisma.

Charisma is the attribute that makes other people go unimaginable lengths for you willingly. Charismatic people are described as those that are not only powerful but are also likable. They are unique, irresistible, and possess every combination that will help them open doors of opportunities.

For some people, charisma as quality may seem like a mystery. These are the kind of people that think some people are born with charisma while others are not. Well, thankfully, this isn't the case. If you wish to develop charisma, you do not have to possess unique genes to build yourself to become a person who has an endearing, powerful, and likable demeanor.

As a result of the fact that charisma is not a magical trait that one cannot easily explain, it can be further broken down to a set of solid and generally nonverbal attitudes that a person can learn, practice, and turn into an attitude as well as a way of life. These attributes are divided into three different categories which are Presence, Power, and Warmth. When a person combines these behaviors effectively, it will result in a strong personal attribute that will attract other people to him or her.

Presence

Have you ever been in a situation where you were talking to someone, but you feel like they are not paying full attention to you? Now how did you feel when you came to that realization? Angry right? Well, it's only natural for you to feel that way. It is quite unfortunate that it is only a few people that can maintain full presence when they are in conversation with other people. This has always been a challenge for so many people for the sole reason that most people have an element of conversational narcissism in them.

It gets even harder with the amount of influence that smartphones have over people in the 21st century. People now struggle to shuffle their attention between the virtual world and the real world. These days, people tend to be only physically present while their attention is with the internet world, which they fully interact with via their phones.

If you walk into a restaurant, you will find people who are seated and are staring into their phones while someone else is seated across the table, but they are not conversing with each other. How funny; the world is indeed becoming a crazy place.

The good news lies in the fact that it is possible for an individual to pull himself from the world of the internet by maintaining a presence with the people that are present with them, giving them their unreserved attention.

When you think of being a charismatic person, you should consider the possibility of making yourself look like an awesome person to other people. The flip side of this quality is that you do not have to sing praises of your unique qualities. The focus should be on making other people feel welcomed and important as they are talking to you and after they have finished interacting with you. You should be able to make them feel good about themselves, much more than they did before they got into the conversation with you.

By investing a large chunk of your mental and your emotional energy on the person you are interacting with, you will be able to create an air of importance and confidence for the other person. Most of the time, what people want is attention, recognition, and acknowledgment.

To put your charisma on display, you don't have to be an outgoing person or an extrovert. Famous technology entrepreneur Elon Musk is often cited as an example of a person who has been able to gain a full grasp of the art of a charismatic presence. Elon Musk is described as an intelligent, very reserved, and quiet person by nature, but he is able to maintain a balance between his introverted nature and a good sense of focus, as well as his presence. This type of person does not need to be all out or be the life of the party to endear people to himself. He would instead concentrate on giving his full, unreserved attention to few people, than being everywhere and around everyone, chatting with them and giving a bit of himself to most of those present at the party. By giving intense attention to a few people, he makes them feel very special. In this case, what charisma offers is not quantity, but quality.

Being able to maintain presence is a simple thing to do, but most times, people find themselves struggling with achieving it. It is not something that can be faked. When you are pretending to be interested in a conversation, it is usually effortless to figure out. If you must be present, you must do so in deed and truth. This is going to demand a lot of willpower to sieve through distractions and place your attention on what the other person has to offer at a particular moment. Just like every other thing in life, it becomes easier to master with time.

Here are some tips to guide you in the art of mastering charismatic presence:

Bring Yourself to the Moment (Mindfulness)

The cradle of presence is in mind. Whenever you are in a conversation with someone, and you feel like your mind may have wandered off somewhere else, you can consider practicing mindfulness exercises to help you bring back your attention to the moment. You should pay attention to those physical sensations of your body that you always easily ignore. This may either be your breath or the feeling that comes with your feet touching the floor. You don't need long hours of meditation on these feelings. You only need a few seconds to return you to the moment that you are currently sharing with the other person.

Ensure That You Are Physically Comfortable

Bringing yourself to be physically present with a person is hard when everything that is going through your mind is how you are so uncomfortable with the shoe you are wearing or how you are not able to sit up because your tight pants may just get ripped off. This is why you need to be as comfortable as possible. Always wear clothes that are very comfortable and well fitted. Besides the fact that it will make you feel at peace with yourself, well-fitted clothes will also make you look better.

You can also increase your physical comfort by getting adequate sleep or staying away from caffeine; it is better to be calm than to be jittery.

Place Your Mobile Devices on Silence or Put Them Away

This trick has two effects: first, it will help you to avoid the temptation of checking them while you are talking to someone else. Secondly, it will make the person you are talking to know they have your undivided attention and that you are not sharing the time you have with them with your phone. This makes them feel important and would also give you all their attention.

Look at the Person You Are Talking to In the Eye

Several studies have revealed that those who make more eye contact with their audience are thought to have a lot of positive qualities. These qualities include warmth, competence, emotional stability, confidence, sincerity, and honesty. Eye contact does not only help you look appealing to the person you are talking to in every way, but it also boosts the quality of the conversation you are having. With eye contact, there is an increased sense of intimacy in your interactions, and the person who is on the other side will have a sense of positivity towards the exchange; hence, they will feel like they are connected to you in some ways.

You have to note that eye contact may work in helping you to build intimacy with friends, and in other friendly scenarios.

However, research has shown that this may also work against you if you are trying to convince a person that is skeptical about your opinion.

Make Gestures to Show That You Are Listening

Asides making eye contact, body language is another effective way of maintaining a presence. Nodding your head does this trick much more than any other gesture. Note, you have to be careful with these nods as doing it too much will come off as though you are trying too hard to impress the person you are conversing with. This will result in a decrease in your power in the eyes of the other person. Ensure you nod only when it is appropriate, and this will demand that you listen to know when it's okay to nod.

Ask Questions for Clarification

Asking questions to clarify issues or things you are not sure about is a very easy way to show someone that you were there with them as they were talking. For instance, you may ask questions like, "when you say 'hype,' you mean what?" Another way to ask clarifying questions is by paraphrasing what the person has already said. For instance, "You mean you have the recipe for the bread? Am I getting you?"

When you are in casual scenes or conversations, you can also ask questions like "what is your favorite movie?" or "What do you consider as the hardest part of being a teacher?

Generally, people tend to enjoy it when they reflect on such questions and when they answer them.

Don't fidget

When you fidget, it gives the other person the impression that you are not comfortable or satisfied with the conversation and that they would rather be elsewhere. So, when you are talking to someone, be careful not to fondle your thumbs or play with something in front of you. You should also be careful not to excessively look around the place to see what else is going on around you. This will make it look as if you unsettled, and it will make the other person think you are looking out for a better chance than you already have.

Don't Focus on Finding a Response to the Person As They Are Still Talking

People tend to do this easily. In fact, almost everyone does this. Our innate selfishness is always ready to chip in response as soon as there is a chance to do so. Unfortunately, the fact that you are already thinking of what you are going to say indicates that you are not paying full attention to whatever the other person has to say. It is only natural to want to have something to say before you say it, but it is ideal for working through the response you are going to give as you are giving it. Savor every moment that you have to pause and enjoy the conversation to the fullest.

Pause for Two Seconds Before You Respond

You can break-in at the very moment the last speaker pauses or immediately after he has stopped talking. It shows that you were already thinking of what you were going to say even before he or she stopped talking, instead of paying attention to what they were saying. Non-verbal communication always seems to be more effective than verbal communication so you can make use of the following tricks to prove that you are present in the conversation:

When a person is done talking to you, first try to make use of your facial expression to show that you have assimilated what the person said to you. You can then make a striking statement to give the person's speech the consideration that it deserves. After you have done this for about two seconds, you can now give your answer.

You may consider the following sequence:

· They finish making their statements.

· You absorb their speech with your face.

· React also with your face.

· Then you can finally give your answer.

Power

Charismatic people come off as very powerful people, but it does not always mean that they hold strong leadership positions or are successful entrepreneurs. The reality is that most times, the most influential people are found in the humblest sides of life.

By the mere fact that powerful people can influence the world around them, they find it easier to get things done or give the impression that they can get things done. What charismatic people do is to attract people into their circle like a magnet. Their power is the core of this magnetic force and the primary point of attraction.

Looking back to the times when humans lived in caves, the survival of a person could be dependent on being friendly with bigwigs that were at that time, at the top of the social hierarchy. During those times, those bigwigs had the power to give protection and give assurance for food, spouses, and general survival. To be able to get more latch into these types of people, the human brain further developed to interpret body language and other markers that can easily indicate the status of a person, as well as power.

The good thing is that humans had since moved past this era several centuries ago.

However, people are still attracted to those who possess valuable resources or people who seem to know how to get those resources. Though the survival of humans may no longer depend mainly on the connection one has with such people, the possibility of one having access to higher personal and professional opportunities can depend on such connections.

Therefore, it is important to note that every one of the three components of charisma must work together if one must come to the point of magnetism. Although you may appear to be the most pleasant and the best listener in the room, if you do not have power, you are likely to be merely seen as the nice guy or worse still, seen as a desperate person This may look harsh, but the truth is that people place value on your presence and warmth according to the amount of power they think you have. Look at it this way: if you have done an excellent job and you get complimented by a co-worker and the manager of the company, which of the compliment will be valued? For most people, the compliment from the manager will be more appreciated because he is the one with more power.

On the other hand, a person who has power and is devoid of warmth and presence will not pass for a charismatic person. When a person is powerful but lacks these qualities, he will be considered as an impressive and important person, but he will appear to be aloof, nonchalant, arrogant, and cold.

Increasing your Charismatic Power

Increasing your charismatic power may seem difficult at first. It may look the same way as applying for a job that demands experience before you can be hired, but you need to secure the job before you can get the required experience. You need to keep in mind that charisma is all about the perception that other people have of you; you don't need a large amount of money or know so many influential people to be charismatic.

To gain power, you have to give the impression that you already have that power. This is mostly a 'fake it until you make it situation.' When people can perceive your supposed charismatic power, they will invite you into their circle of influence, and then, you will gain power in the real sense of it. This will equip you to practice charismatic power by building a more virtuous circle, capable of earning you more success.

Giving the impression of power boils down to boosting those things that humans naturally consider when they are trying to determine the level at which a person possesses power. This may be in terms of body language or appearance. Below are ways you can boost your charismatic power:

Enhance Your Confidence

The possession of power begins from the mind. If you are confident in the fact that you are powerful, other people will start to feel the same way about you. Being able to reassure yourself will give you an aura that cannot be easily resisted, and this will attract people to you because they will want to know more about you. Building confidence is crucial to gain power, and it is noteworthy to understand that the core of confidence lies in one's ability to master it.

A person who can gain expertise in any skill or area of knowledge will come off as one who has resources at his disposal. In the same light, he will come off as one who has enough willpower and perseverance to go into the deepest parts of a particular subject. When you can gain mastery of a specific topic, it will also boost the way you look, feel, and carry yourself.

Know A Little About So Many Topics/Things

As a plus to your self-worth, you should not only focus on your area of expertise. You should also strive to know as much as you can about different subjects. If you must be that man who can influence the world, intelligence should be one of your greatest fortes. The more you can join in conversations and add to them, the smarter you will be perceived, and the more likable you will become.

To gain a wide range of knowledge, you have to keep reading and never stop learning. With every chance you get, learn something new.

Be Physically Fit

When people meet you for the first time, the shape of your body is one of the things that they take note of. A person who has a fit, muscular physique comes off as one who is strong. This type of frame sends a signal to the primary parts of the brains of others about your ability to protect and dominate. A physically fit body will also make others perceive you as one who has discipline and can endure pain to achieve a greater goal. This may be the reason why those men who are well-built seem to be wealthier than their obese and skinny counterparts.

Dress for Power

One of the most potent and earliest power cues is how a person is dressed. When you see a military man dressed in his military uniform with ribbons and stars on his shoulder, the first thing that will readily come to your mind is 'authority.' To create this impression, the military person does not have to scream it at the top of his voice or show off his stars. This also goes with the type of regular clothing you wear. While it is okay to dress modest, studies have shown that high-status dressing can influence other people.

Asides the fact that your dressing makes you appear to others as a powerful person when you dress well, your confidence will get boosted, and you will even begin to feel powerful yourself. When you feel more powerful, you do things as one who is powerful, and this will make others perceive you that way. This is known as the virtuous charismatic circle.

Act as the Big "Gorilla"

Asides clothing, there is also another feature that influences the way other people look at you in terms of power, and that is body language.

This is the paralinguistic cues that show the power, and it deals mostly with the amount of space a person makes use of. As you may have already pictured in your head, powerful people usually make use of more space than those who are not. Powerful people are like 'big gorillas.'

If you wish to boost the viewpoint of other people as regards the power you possess, you have to figure out ways to increase the amount of space you take up subtly. Try draping your hand across the back of your chair or sit on the desk instead of sitting behind it when a colleague comes to have a chat with you in the office.

Take on Power Poses

This is quite related to being the big gorilla. Power poses means that you are going to place your body in a way that will portray power. The most popular power pose is putting one's hand akimbo by making the hands rest on the waist. This kind of posture is very common among superheroes. You can also consider resting back on your chair and placing your hand at the back of your head. Putting your feet on the table wouldn't be a bad idea. Whichever you do, don't overdo it.

During a meeting, you can decide to portray power in the room by standing up and leaning forward. While you do this, your hands should be rested on the table before you.

This will make you look like the most important person in the room at that time, and you are going to carry that air of authority with you afterward.

You can also try to lift your arms straight into the air like one who has just made a touchdown pass to decide the fate of a game. Though one cannot clearly state at what point this pose is more likely to work, it can be imbibed into your everyday life in a way that will not look too weird.

Interestingly, all of these poses will not only make you look powerful to other people, but they will also make you feel powerful.

Merely assuming a power pose for a few minutes can increase your testosterone levels and reduce the level of cortisol in your body. This will increase your level of confidence and reduce your stress level. By feeling more confident, you will begin to act more powerfully. This, on its own, is another feature of the charismatic virtuous circle.

Take Charge of Your Environment

People usually have a level of self-assurance, ease, and power when they are in familiar terrain. When a person is familiar with his environment, he gains a level/sense of control, and this is what boosts his level of confidence. It is for reasons like this that many organizations will prefer to choose their location even before they begin with negotiations.

Both sides of the divide typically want to feel at home, so they both want a familiar terrain.

Note, you may not always be the one to choose your environment, so you have to learn to be at home in every new location. You may ask, how is it possible to be comfortable in a room that you are entering for the first time? There are some little things which experts recommend for getting control of one's surroundings. For instance, you walk into a restaurant, try to rearrange the things on the table you are going to sit on. You may choose to move the jug or the saltshaker.

This may seem like a funny idea, but when you do this, you unconsciously have an idea that you are in control of the things that are around you. This will make you feel confident and magnetic. In your everyday life, you can look out for little and polite ways of being in charge of your environment. The result of this will be amazing.

Say Few Things and Say Them Slowly

Powerful people do not only occupy physical space but also, they take up space in conversations. This is a bit of a paradox because it does not demand that you hog upon the time you have to speak. Unlike people who are not as influential, powerful people are prone to speaking fewer words. By the mere fact that they make sure that their words are scarce, powerful people add a lot of value to the words they speak. Whenever they talk, people will want to listen to them. You can try out this tip; being less of the chatty type and being more laconic with the way you talk will help you a lot.

When in conversations, powerful people fill up space with silence. Unlike most people, awkward silence isn't so awkward to powerful people. As a matter of fact, they savor those silent moments.

These types of people have come to the understanding that people naturally want to fill up silent gaps, and it is the nervousness that comes with wanting to do this that they devour some strategic or useful piece of information. This is the reason why investigators, negotiator, and interviewers rely on silence to bring out the vulnerability of the other person to capitalize on it.

Talking slowly is also another way in which people consume space in conversations. People who speak fast portray a sense of anxiety and nervousness, while those who speak slowly displays a sense of thoughtfulness, intelligence, and calmness that powerful people possess. Powerful people speak slowly while the less powerful ones talk fast because if they are not fast with the things they have to say, people will not listen to them. This is the basic rule of human nature. Play a record of yourself talking, and you will be quite surprised by how fast you talk. If you make an effort to slow down, you will soon master it. Although in the beginning, it is going to seem as though you are talking too slowly, but once you can master it, you are going to sound normal and even excellent.

Improve Your Poise

One of the common traits of powerful people is composure. There is a sense of grace and stillness in them, and they have poise.

Powerful people will not be caught nodding excessively as a sign of being submissive, and they will not be fidgety as a result of being nervous. Powerful people will not be found in need of verbal fillers like 'um' and 'uh,' so next time you have to interact with people, you should try to be as natural as possible while you remain focused on being still. You should nod at intervals to indicate your presence, but don't turn yourself to a lizard by nodding all the time. Make sure your hand is still and do not tap your feet excessively.

Warmth

A person who emanates warmth is generally perceived by others as one who is caring, easy-going, and empathetic because people feel comfortable being around them, and they are also at peace with them. Every human being wishes to be understood, acknowledged, and taken care of. A warm spirit takes care of all of these. It satisfies the craving of wanting to gain solid grounds in our beings from childhood to adulthood. Warmth is taking care of a person when they haven't asked to be taken care of, or caring for an individual despite having messed up. Warmth is giving a friend a shoulder to lean on or giving kudos when it is due.

Regardless of how old a person is or how independent they have become, everyone appreciates the feeling of being cared for or being at peace with someone.

The same with power and presence, warmth is important to balance all the other elements as it also cannot work effectively on its own. A person who has power but is devoid of warmth will be perceived as cold and arrogant, while one who has warmth without power will be seen as a weak person who seeks validation by wanting to please everyone.

Amongst the three elements of charisma, warmth is usually the most difficult to fake. Typically, people can manage to convince others that they are present even though their minds seem to have wandered a little bit. They can also easily act like they have got their life in one piece when the reality is that they are still struggling to achieve their goals. People somehow manage to figure out when a person is faking warmth and when they figure this out, they seem to withdraw a little bit from such people because they have been made to assume that they are showing a fake version of themselves.

This element of charisma will easily backfire if those around you can figure out that the reason why you are giving it is that you wish to get something from them. This is the reason why people tend to dislike marketers who try to come off as nice because they are desperate to close a deal to secure their paycheck.

This is not to say that it is bad to want something from people; if we were true to ourselves, we would all agree that the major point of charisma is the ability to influence others to do something in our favor. Regardless of whatever the case may be, whether you are trying to have them buy a particular good or services, or go on a date with you, the point is that you shouldn't seek to influence people solely for your selfish gains.

If warmth must be genuine, it has to be based on something that goes beyond selfish reasons. It must be as a result of one's satisfaction with life and as a result of empathy and curiosity about others. A person who has genuine warmth will not hesitate to know people from different works of life. This type of person has the mindset that despite they are not able to get what they need from their interaction with the other person, they will still be grateful to have met the person because they feel their interaction with such people is worth their time and effort.

If warmth must be effective in creating an endearing spirit, the outward attitudes that show a sense of warmth to other people must come from a powerful, yet the indescribable quality that comes from a genuine heart. The root of charismatic warmth begins from the crux of an individual.

Creating Warmth from Within

There are some people that being with them is intoxicating. These people have a way of making you feel important and notice. At the end of a conversation with such people, they will linger in your thoughts; you don't necessarily have to be in a romantic relationship with them to feel this way. These people have warmth from within, which they give to make you have these feelings.

People that create warmth from within have the power to captivate your attention. They make you notice them when they speak, make you listen to them, and make you open to their influence. Spending a little time with them will always make your mood brighter. People with warmth are always enjoyed, sought-after, trusted, and influential and remembered. This magic of creating warmth doesn't lie in what they say or how they make you feel it lies in two practices, and anyone can learn it.

If you wish to create warmth from within yourself, there are two ways to go about it:

Show Gratitude

A heart that is full of gratitude is a happy one. Research has shown that those who show gratitude every day are happy people. People who show gratitude are more positive than those who do not show gratitude.

To create a grateful heart, you can choose to write those things that you are truly grateful for. Every day of your life, once you can portray a spirit of gratitude, you will be able to put the things that bother you into perspective. This will help you to stay relaxed by having a spirit of contentment which reflects in your interaction with others and will also put them at ease when they are with you.

Be Empathetic

Empathy can be said to be a "fellow feeling." This is the most important feature that can help one to live a healthy social and political life. If you must develop charismatic warmth, this is a crucial factor to consider. Generally, people appreciate being understood, and it is empathy that helps us to put ourselves in other people's shoes to feel the way they are feeling.

Certainly, it is not easy to develop empathy because there are a lot of things to discourage it in modern times, and these things can make you cynical about the state of humans. Regardless, it is possible to develop it.

Here are some tips that will help you to reduce this cynicism and gain more empathy for other people:

See Others as Your Brothers and Sisters

This is a mindset that has roots in religious beliefs which holds that all humans were created by the same God, or in the scientific theory that believes humans have their origin from a certain place in the African continent. This scientific belief also holds that everyone is made of the same stardust.

Whether religious or scientific, one thing that is arguably certain is that all humans are cosmically connected. This may sound cheesy, but the thought that everyone is family members that are journeying through the same path will help you to show more compassion to others even at times when you need to feel otherwise.

Interact with Others Physically

Studies have shown that college students had become less empathetic than their counterparts over the years. What could be the reason for this decline? The answer to this may be in the fact that people now interact less physically as humans now operate as disembodied individuals on the internet. There is a lot of power in physical interactions; the mere sight of people's facial expressions is enough to trigger a feeling of empathy in people.

When these physical cues are not available, it becomes possible to portray evil motives towards other people as these motives can easily go unchecked/unpunished. You may want to consider stepping away from your keyboard often and step into the real world to interact with people. If you can do this, you will gain another perspective of humans asides the terrible viewpoint you had of them as a result of your interactions online.

Think of a Different Story about Those That Annoy You

As you are rushing to meet up with your interview, the chances are that you, at one point, had to cut someone off while you were driving. Though you hate to have done that, you tell yourself that it is something you had to do to secure the job. When the tables are turned, and you are the one that was being cut off, you judge the person who had done that to be wicked. This is because it is easy to make excuses for our misdemeanors because we think they are things we had to do, while we consider the same attitudes from others as a flaw in their character. This does not have to be so. You can try to be a bit more compassionate about others the same way you are to yourself, by imagining the reasons why they possibly acted rudely or were so annoying to you.

Be Curious About Others

If you must put yourself in other people's shoes, you must first try to know them. This is the reason why you have to ask questions for clarification to see things from their points of view and also, to be able to know the reason why they have become how they are. With every meeting comes the possibility of getting to know about the human experience. Do not miss any chance.

The more you can develop empathy, the more you find out that every human is going through one hard stuff or the other. When you can realize the fact that there is a struggle for every man, you will feel the need to be a source of relieve for others. You will naturally want to be that person who lightens the burdens of others by making them feel understood, safe, and tranquilized even within the shortest time.

Showing Warmth to Others

Since one cannot easily fake warmth because it is something a person must nurture from within, let's consider the roles of our outward attributes to this element of charisma.

First, we have to ask ourselves if it is possible for a person to have a good heart but not good at showing kindness to other people. Sometimes, people are aware of the fact that they are too careless about emotions, although they will like to think that they are good people. The truth is that having inner warmth alone isn't enough.

One's ability to show this warmth to those around them also matters a lot.

Also, the level of warmth a person shows on the outside influences the warmth he feels on the inside. This is a virtuous circle. The more warmth you show to others, the more warmth you feel inside, and this is what makes you warm towards others. As a matter of fact, if you can show warmth, you will also be developing your inner warmth at a quick pace and even more effectively. You don't have to wait to feel like you are an empathetic person before you start acting like one. Naturally, you become what you act as. So, you should make efforts to work on your behavior and your mindset simultaneously. They both work hand in hand.

You don't have to worry yourself with thoughts of appearing fake as a result of acting warmly before you actually feel it inside. What matters most is the fact that you have a good motive for your actions.

Below, I will be discussing some behaviors that you can easily pull off if you are not awkward about them, and if you are not doing them exaggeratedly. They are easy ways in which you can put your best foot forward with people you interact with. If you are trying it for the first time, you may feel a bit awkward about it, but you don't have to worry because you have to begin somewhere.

Once you start practicing them, the charismatic warmth circle will begin, and with time, it will register as an entirely genuine act.

Consider Yourself as a Host

Imagine a scenario when you have people visiting you at home. What are those things that you do naturally as a host? Certainly, the most important thing to you is such cases is the comfort of your guests. Now try to imbibe this mindset in your interactions with others. Whenever you are thinking of yourself as a host, you would easily figure out what you can do to make other people at ease.

Give Sincere Compliments

Nothing works better than a sincere compliment in tensed situations. It is capable of strengthening relationships and melting hearts. It is too bad that people tend to be very stingy with kind words. It may not be your style, but you have to learn how to give compliments as it will make a lot of things easier. You can also learn ways of accepting compliments also.

Your Voice Should Reflect More Warmth

Naturally, our voice carries a lot of emotions, and it is not only reflected in the way we say things, but it also reflects in the tone with which we say them, as well as the pitch we use.

When we are angry, we tend to speak in loud and harsh tones, while kindness and warmth are reflected in softer and milder tones to imbibe warmth in your tone. Instead, you can take the easy route of smiling when you are talking.

This communicates a sense of instant warmth. This will be a lot helpful in non-physical communications like when you are talking on the phone. Though you do not have body language and facial expressions at your disposal in such situations, you can use your voice, which at that point is your only tool to communicate warmth.

Offer Your "Kind Eyes"

Some people have what can be described as kind eyes. This kind of look is reflected in the gaze that people give, which makes others at peace, understood, and accepted. However, it is possible for someone to have this kind of eyes, yet not be a good person; these are the kind of people that can switch from being nice from afar to being a beast when you get closer to them. Although your world may be crumbling right in front of them, they will give you a look that will make you feel like everything is alright, while they could have actually helped you to save the situation.

A person's eyes are the pathway to his soul, and when you have kind eyes, it reflects the goodness of your heart.

However, there are ways in which a person can boost the kindness that is reflected in his eyes in order for it to truly depict his inner warmth. To have a kind heart, you can switch your look to a milder focus. Instead of giving a squint or a stare like you are about to punch the person that is in front of you, you can actually relax your gaze and broaden your focus. When you are able to feel like your face is relaxed around your eyes, you are most likely to have been able to achieve 'kind eyes.'

Anticipate Needs

You may always choose to give something to people without them asking for it. This shows that you care about them, and you are looking out for them. For example, you may choose to get your colleague at work a cup of coffee because you feel it is going to help them. Think about offering your jacket to someone because you think they might need it on a cold winter morning or simply giving someone a hand.

Offer a Warm Drink

A warm drink has a magical feel that gives people warm feelings, so you see, offering a cup of coffee might have a bit of a psychological impact on the person you gave it to as it will also generate a feeling of warmth towards you. Well, this may be the reason why coffee shops are a top choice for business meetings and first dates.

Give a Firm/Good Handshake

One of the best ways to influence warmth in another person is by touch. Though you may have to/want to respect people's space and not touch them in ways that may be considered inappropriate (especially in a flirty manner). Because there are rules, a handshake may be the most appropriate way to make skin-to-skin contact, so you may want to make good use of it with every opportunity you get.

If you wish to give your handshake a boost that will induce warmth, you can extend your index finger to the inner part of the wrist of the other person while you are clasping your hands. According to some experts in communication, when you touch the pulse point of a person while you are shaking hands with them, they will feel a sense of connection towards you.

Try to Know the Effort That Other People Are Putting into Things

There is some sort of little martyr in everyone, and we all want people to take note of the trouble that we faced to get something done. While we all have these cravings, it may be a little awkward to list them out. The best way to go about acknowledging the efforts of others is by having them tell you about it by asking questions that will give them the chance to talk about it.

If, for example, a friend has driven long hours to see you, you can ask about the things he had to pass through or those he had to forfeit to see you.

Make Them Feel at Ease

People will always be grateful for those that help them avoid the feeling of being alone. You can easily show warmth by introducing people to your circle and having them join in on your conversations or ideas. You should also learn how to be able to master the art of taking charge of conversations by learning how to engage in small talks effectively. People always like to have someone at a particular gathering whom they are sure will be able to keep the conversation running.

Remember Details like Dates and Anniversaries

Everyone likes the feeling that comes with someone else remembering their birthdays. This will go a long way to help someone feel loved and important. This does not have to do with merely sending texts or posting birthday messages on the person's Facebook wall. Going extra miles to send cards or sending emails will count for so much more. This will not only be an avenue to wish them happy birthdays, but it will also be an opportunity to catch up with their welfare. This also goes for other milestones and anniversaries.

It is also possible to show warmth by remembering other details like the name of a person and that of their loved ones. Asking after the welfare of the people they care about will mean a lot to them as well.

Give Thoughtful Gifts

This is not talking about gift cards, and it does not also have to be big gifts. Thoughtful gifts are simply those gifts that will show that you paid attention to the needs of another person. When a person you care about mentions what he likes and what he is interested in having, you can simply lock the idea away in your head, or you can even make a note about it. They will definitely be happy if, at a later time, you come up with that same thing they have mentioned that they would like to have.

Also, these gifts may be something they make a habit of acquiring, say a pack of the person's favorite drink. It would make the person happy to have you show up unexpectedly with something he/she truly likes.

Sort Things Out

If someone is facing a problem and you can help them take care of it, do so without hesitation. If, for example, they have a question that you do not have an answer to, you can simply say you don't know, but you will help them find out. If there is a task that you can assist them in, give them a hand.

You know there is a deadline to meet, so you have offered to help. This will mean a whole lot to the person.

Remember that you do not have to be a pushover to convey warmth, but if there is any way you can help a friend with your time or expertise, do so. You can always do your best to do something that will, at least, lighten someone else's burden.

Be Liberal with Appreciations

It is possible to show warmth without being physically present. A simple thank you note is one of the best ways to do this. There is no single time that can be considered a bad time to show appreciation. A simple thank you note will make people realize that you noticed their effort, and you took out time to acknowledge the fact that they have done something or to acknowledge their place in your life. You may possibly pen this down by hand and put it in an envelope. The receiver will certainly smile when they receive it.

Notes

Chapter 4.   Self-Esteem vs Self-Confidence

S elf-esteem is often described as self-judgment. It refers to the overall notion of personal value or self-worth. It's comprised of various ideas regarding oneself, such as the assessment of appearance, emotions, behaviors and principles. Essentially, self-esteem is simply a measure of how much you appreciate yourself, and how well you can operate throughout the day, despite the external and internal hardships you will face.

High overall self-esteem is critical to achieving a harmonious life. It's the driver which underpins all positive behavior patterns. You can't achieve anything without first believing that you deserve to have it, and this is exclusively linked to your self-worth. It's a little different compared to say pure confidence for instance. There's a slight but significant difference between the two.

Some would argue that we are merely debating semantics here, but I determine confidence as more of a state trait. It's more closely linked with competence in a given area or task. We all feel confident in some settings, but not in others. Confidence is typically determined by proficiency which comes with practice and repetition. Do you feel confident when you first get behind the wheel of a car?

Do you feel comfortable giving a speech in front of 50 colleagues for the first time? Of course not. But drive every day for 10 years or give 100 speeches and it's a different story.

Self-esteem, however, runs deeper than this. It goes beyond situational states of competence. It transcends any situation you may find yourself in. It pertains to the internal feelings and emotional components of a person's personality, which I described previously. In this sense, increasing your overall self-worth is a very worthwhile thing to do, as it positively affects every area of your life. It's a tide which raises all boats so to speak.

I would argue that there is no downside to ever increasing levels of self-esteem. You simply love yourself and the others around you just that much more each day. Some will talk about achieving a level of balance, but I would suggest they are again referring to self-confidence, or more accurately, grandiose levels of self-importance.

There is definitely a downside to taking yourself too seriously, but also not seriously enough. Operating at either end of this extreme confidence spectrum can be detrimental in opposing ways. This is why I want to touch upon this briefly before moving onto the specific tenets of developing true self-worth. In an ideal situation, those with high levels of self-esteem would also have healthy levels of self-confidence. But that's not always the case.

The Importance of Balance When it Comes to Confidence

People with extremely low levels of self-confidence often deal with frequent feelings of defeat and depression. They tend to get pulled into situations wherein they make bad choices, plain and simple. They settle for unhealthy relationships and fail to be the best versions of themselves. Something always holds them back from succeeding, due mainly to the lack of necessary self-beliefs which trigger self-sabotaging behavior.

On the other hand, people with an overblown sense of self-confidence can prove to be very obnoxious and oftentimes intolerable. They tend to think of themselves as better than everyone else, which prevents them from cultivating healthy personal and professional relationships alike. They refuse to admit when they are wrong and habitually blame everyone but themselves for their own shortcomings.

Again, there's a fine line here. I often hear people say things like "I'm often wrong, but never in doubt". On one hand, this serves as a great success mindset to have. It allows a person to push forward with little to no distractions in their mind. It affords a focus critical to getting big goals achieved. However, it can be highly annoying to the surrounding people when a person gets too entrenched in a position without ever taking a self-critical view on things.

These people are extremely competitive and always striving to get ahead of the pack. They view material and monetary success as their main source of happiness, but their attitude simply makes true happiness elusive. Unsurprisingly, all of the aforementioned traits make it very difficult to establish affectionate and healthy relationships with those around them. They view everyone as an opponent to be overthrown in the continual competition of life.

Those who exhibit low self-esteem, on the other hand, do the exact opposite. They fail to see their worth, they cannot acknowledge their capabilities, and these insecurities always loom in every situation they find themselves in. They are constantly fearful of failing which holds them back. They take a different route, but ultimately end up in the same place of unhappiness.

A healthy self-confidence can be found somewhere in the middle of these extremes. It's having realistic confidence in one's own skills and abilities. It's in reaching an "unconscious competence" level of proficiency of a task. You know exactly what you can and cannot do, in any particular moment. However, you are not inhibited by this. You are aware of your strengths and weaknesses, and you know how to maximize them to get closer to your ultimate goals.

Healthy levels of self-confidence ensure a person feels secure enough to withstand unfavorable events and failures.

It's worth noting, that maintaining this kind of state takes a lifetime of work and dedication to tasks. There will be moments when insecurities can arise, especially in competitive contexts. The mind is never static, so the key to self-confidence therein lies in having the constant motivation to learn how life's adversities can be overcome. This takes a continual effort to push the boundaries of one's own comfort zone.

How Self-Esteem Develops

So, having explored the notion of overall self-confidence, it's now time to switch gears. It's time to assess what it means to have true self-esteem or self-worth (I'll use these terms interchangeably as they are generally describing the same thing).

Self-esteem is an essential element for maintaining your overall well-being. It will play a significant role in our attempts to form healthy and positive relationships as we go through life. In fact, our view of our adult self is highly influenced by how we lived as children. It goes back to infancy and gradually develops as time passes by. A healthy self-esteem can be established early on in a child's life simply by making him or her feel safe, accepted, and genuinely loved. It is long been known that virtually all of our personality traits and feelings of self-worth are developed during this time.

From the age of 2 years up until around 6-7, children are like sponges, they absorb everything.

EEG pattern studies indicate that they spend much of this time in high frequency theta brain wave states. This explains why they can learn at rapid rates, even picking up multiple languages simultaneously with relative ease.

A friend of mine visited Amsterdam a few years back and was surprised to find she could loosely understand the locals when they are talking to one another. On returning to the States she told the story to her parents, who reminded her that she spent most of her days as a toddler with a nanny from Holland. It turned out this lady used to speak Dutch to my friend when she looked after her. But English when her parents got home from work. The remnants of the language had remained in her subconscious mind all of this time.

More critically though, we also attribute meaning to things and situations during those formative years which forms our base paradigms for viewing the world. How are parents and siblings react to us has a monumental impact on our behavior into adolescence and then adult life. Things which often need to be re-visited in order to rectify deeply held notions of self-worth, or lack thereof.

For the majority of people I meet, low levels of self-esteem can almost always be tracked back to some form of neglect as a child. Or some form of miss appropriation of meaning from menial events when growing up.

In fact, everything in childhood will affect a person's eventual level of elf-esteem. Each time a child tries to do and learn new things is an opportunity for them to develop higher degrees of self-worth, such as:

- Learning new concepts in school

- Acquiring new skills (art, music, sports, cooking, etc.)

- Making new friends

- Getting feedback on behavior, good and bad

Children who know how to feel good about themselves will grow into adults who are confident enough to try out new things. They will know how to deal with mistakes, and failure will not prevent them from getting up and trying again. I write about this re-contextualization more thoroughly within "Jealousy: A Psychologists Guide". But it's certainly safe to say that this stems from childhood by and large.

Did your parents ever warn you of the dangers in life? Did they ever stress the importance of looking both ways before crossing the street? They likely did, and they are well within their rights to do so.

Protecting a child is paramount to any parent, but what they are subconsciously communicating is "the world is a scary place, watch out for dangers at every turn". It's no wonder we grow up not ever wanting to take the slightest of risks.

If you read some of the autobiographies of the world's most successful entrepreneurs, they all have one thing in common.

Their parents did the opposite of the above. Richard Branson grew up on a farm in the British countryside wherein his mother would instruct him to go out and find adventure each day. To go out and explore the world. It's no coincidence that his net worth is now north of $5 billion.

Dr. Benjamnin Spock was one of the first American pediatricians to study the psychoanalysis of children. He wrote a book in 1946 titled "The Common Sense Book of Baby & Childcare" which fast became a best seller. Among other great advice contained within the book, the central theme was predominantly based around how to communicate with children. Specifically, how to negotiate requests and never to say "No" to them. But rather explore the avenues of their questions and the implications they might have. To get them to think more critically, but importantly, so they don't grow up with negative connotations to being turned down for what they want.

Studies show that parents who implemented these techniques went on to raise some of the most well-rounded and successful children measured for every metric of success. By contrast, children who develop low self-esteem during these formative years will often feel unsure of themselves. They may always harbor a feeling of inadequacy and be more vulnerable to mistreatment later in life. They are more prone to bullying and poor treatment from others in high school and later on within the workplace. They don't handle mistakes and set-back nearly as well as they might.

That being said, none of this is an excuse for continual bad behavior and poor performance. Yes, much of our mental patterns, including those feelings of self-worth are anchored to our early years. But they are NOT set in stone. We can certainly do something about them with a little effort and the correct guidance. While negative thoughts and self-talk is not something that can't be unlearned overnight, we can work on reversing this trend.

Notes

Chapter 5.   Confidence Builders That You Can Include In Your Daily Life

Your mind is more powerful than you realize. Your thoughts are what create your emotions, emotions your actions and your actions are ultimately your life. People who display an excellent level of confidence are better in control of their minds and ultimately their lives.

There are things we can learn from people who display great confidence and we can mirror these actions in our own daily lives without much hassle at all if you are willing to apply yourself and are committed to achieving self-confidence and a skill that will allow you to make your way to the top of the ladder.

Keep your eye on the prize at all times and don't let anyone or anything distract you from your goal. Formulate a plan to reach your goal and go for it. Don't overthink the situation and create unnecessary obstacles.

Confident people maintain a positive outlook. They expect good things to happen to them and as a result, they do. Positive vibes breed and attract positive vibes.

Expectation is a tool that is powerful and if used consistently and unwaveringly, the results are spectacular.

People who display great confidence act and speak in a way that allows you to believe that they have already achieved their goals when in fact they have not. Their belief in themselves and their abilities is so great that there can be no other outcome.

Confident people know how to use their words and speech. They speak with intent, make their point, what they say is what is going to happen and they are not prepared to accept anything less.

Confident people listen to what others have to say but they do not let what is said affect how they feel, their opinions or the goals. They are not distracted by what others say and frankly don't care either. They have set a goal, created a plan and they will complete it.

Confident people are quite happy to decline offers or requests from others to take on tasks if it is going to affect the energy and time they have for their own priorities. They know what is important and they are going to achieve it.

People who are confident do not brag about their accomplishments. Arrogance and confidence must not be confused. If you are confident in your work then allow your work to speak rather than vocalize it. Your work will say so much more than your words ever could.

Failure is inevitable at some point in everybody's life. You cannot fear failure as it could be the reason that you never reach your full potential. Confident people are confident even in failure as they know this storm will pass and they will once again be on top. Failure is a learning curve and you should take whatever you can from the experience.

Always bear in mind that people are not born confident and those rich and powerful people pasted all over our television screens, were not born that way. They were all once normal people just like you but they believed in themselves and their abilities. Confidence must be practiced daily, the more you practice, the easier it will be to maintain a confident and positive attitude. A lifetime of practice is what it takes, there is no reaching the end in this game, confidence will grow and prosper as long as you keep the attitude and positive mind frame.

Exercise for Confidence

You should never underestimate the value of exercise in promoting a general feeling of well-being and boosting your confidence. Without self-confidence, you are more like to take a passive approach to tasks and challenges that life throws your way.

You may have a treasure of valuable ideas or information but without the confidence to speak out and act out, nobody is ever going to realize your brilliance. Exercise is a magical tool that can be used to promote a healthier self-image and boost your confidence in every way.

Exercising allows you to feel well physically, the healthier you feel physically, the healthier you will feel mentally. Your energy levels are boosted and you feel as if you can take on any challenge and obstacle in your path. Feeling great physically and mentally will foster a positive outlook on life and you will feel strong enough emotionally to pursue a lifelong, personal goals.

A negative self-image means that you are not happy with how you look and this leads to a very low self-esteem. If you aren't happy with how you look, you won't be happy with the person you are and this negative attitude will seep into every part of your life. How you act, speak, and react will all be results of your negative self-image. Someone with such a negative self-image will definitely not volunteer their opinions or even wish to stand out from the crowd in any way. Exercising can help to improve your self-image. It can result in weight loss and if that isn't forthcoming, toning your body will improve the appearance that you so dislike. You must also remember that exercise encourages the production of serotonin and this chemical is that wonder chemical that really makes you feel good.

Seeing changes and developments in your body through exercise will boost your self-image and your confidence will follow suit.

Increasing your physical strength has positive effects on your mental strength. Few people realize just how much their bodies can handle and when you finally do, your confidence is increased tenfold. Regular, daily exercise will yield results and some of those results will be noticeable on a daily basis. Physically seeing the positive results will boost your confidence each and every day. It is a wonderful moment when you realize that hard work does pay off and you will begin to implement that at every opportunity you can and show off your new found confidence and belief in your own abilities.

Exercising encourages you to set goals and to work towards achieving them. The sense of accomplishment that you receive through meeting small goals is extremely rewarding. Each time you set a goal and you reach it; your sense of confidence will be boosted. You are capable and you will begin to believe in your abilities with each passing milestone.

Exercise is a wonderful way to reduce stress. When you exercise your brain released feel good chemicals that leave you high on life. Relieved of stress, you are able to move through life happier, more relaxed and focused on your goals. Exercise should be done regularly in order to obtain the desired results.

Without the weight of stress hanging over you, you are able to face challenges calmly and with clear thoughts and you are better able to manage daily life. In this state, you know that you are in control of your emotions and you are the one who will decide your own fate. Tackling obstacles in this frame of mind will definitely yield results and this will boost your confidence endlessly.

Exercise boosts your brain functioning and cognitive functioning. Exercise is food for your brain and allows your brain access to oxygen and nutrients which it needs in order to function properly. Exercise allows you to feel alert and focused and tasks presented are easily dealt with. Exercise improves your mental function, which in turn allows you to complete tasks efficiently and with ease, and this is what ultimately results in the increase of your confidence. Mental and physical wellness enable you with the tools you need to succeed and become the confident person you were born to be.

Exercise is a great way to stay in shape, feed your brain and obtain the level of self-confidence that will encourage you to greatness. Feeling great physically and mentally is the perfect way to ensure that you are on top of your game and ready to take on challenges with a clear head, focus, determination and the knowledge that you can do it, even if it seems impossible at times, you can do it and you will.

Notes

Chapter 6.   Communication Skills

A lot about charisma is in your communication skills. I mean, there's no such thing as a charismatic person who has never interacted with anyone, right?

You don't see any charismatic people inspiring others to action by not reaching out and communicating with others for a reason, and that reason is that charisma is meant to be projected.

You need to project your leadership skills, demonstrate your power, you need to project your image, and you need to persuade people to look at you as someone who inspires them. In order to do that, you have to have great communication skills.

But what does it take to have great communication skills? Isn't it just talking to people? Well, not really.

This chapter is all about the basics. It's the stuff you probably learned from a class in high school but never really paid attention to.

If you're working to build and improve your charisma, then other than your confidence, effective communication is the other big part.

I mean, you can have all the genuine self-confidence in the world, but if you're just being all quiet and not interacting with others, then it's really not going to be worth anything in terms of influencing people.

So, let's start from the foundations then work up to more advanced techniques. If you want the really advanced stuff, check out my book Improve Your People Skills. In that book, I talk less about the basics and more on the advanced communication skills that really attract people. I mean, don't get me wrong, I'll give you lessons here because this is for building your charisma so don't worry.

The main difference between this book and Improve Your People Skills is this book is more focused on you; it's more internal. On the other hand, the other book is more focused on how you make other people feel.

Anyways, let's go back. As I was saying, let's start from the basics then work up to the communication skills you need to build and improve your charisma.

When you "talk" to someone in person, you're really not just speaking words out of your mouth.

There are verbal and nonverbal elements to speech that you need to consider for the overall message to be correctly transferred and understood.

One part of effective communication is learning to match your speech along with your nonverbal cues, then making sure the other person is able to comprehend the message you're trying to give them.

Let me give you an example. If you're from the US, I want you to imagine someone telling you yes, but is shaking their head, face moving side-to-side. What's the message you're getting? Do you take the word "yes," or do you take the gesture indicating "no?"

If you were blind, then the answer you would take is the "yes" because you can't see the head shake. If you were deaf, you would take the "no" head shake because you can't hear. But most people you talk to are neither blind nor deaf. So, your actions have to be in line with the words coming out of your mouth, right?

Another part of effective communication is learning to understand what the other person is really trying to tell you.

Going back to the "yes" with a headshake example, if your friend at work was asked if he finished his project and said yes, while shaking his head behind the boss' back looking at you, then he is probably telling you something like "I wasn't able to finish it, but just say yes."

So there's also context to consider.

Communication is not just giving a message but also receiving a message. Effective communication is giving a message and receiving a message clearly, and in full context of the situation, and that's what I'm going to teach you next.

Verbal Communication

Speech is what most people think about when the word communication is mentioned.

We use our speech so much in communicating with other people that we have tens of thousands of words for different things.

The English alphabet alone has twenty-six different letters representing particular sounds used in English speech. In other cultures like Chinese and Japanese, their "alphabet" is more syllabic with hundreds of symbols representing particular things. In some African dialects, there's even a tongue click represented in English as an exclamation mark.

Given the complexity of speech and all of its components, it's our most powerful and versatile communication tool. Let's discuss each of these components, then move on to the nonverbal elements of communication.

Language

The first component I want to discuss is language because one thing can have different terms used to describe it among the thousands of different languages and dialects in the world.

If you're someone who wants to communicate effectively with someone, you first have to make sure that you speak the same language.

If you only know English like most Americans, then you're okay if you're only ever around people who speak English. However, when you're suddenly in a situation where you're to talk to someone who doesn't know English, then you're automatically placed at a huge disadvantage.

In my job as a company representative, I get exposed to people who speak different languages, but the most common language I encounter is Latin American Spanish.

I never understood Spanish back when I was young, and growing up in California, there were a lot of kids who spoke both Spanish and English, and their parents sometimes only spoke Spanish.

I remember hanging out with at my friend's house after school one time, and his grandma approached me telling me something in Spanish, and I couldn't make out what she was telling me, so I called my friend over.

He then translated for me, telling me that his grandma was asking if I was hungry and wanted some tamales. I said I wasn't hungry, but I would love to try their tamales, which my friend translated back to his grandma.

If I knew how to speak Spanish, I wouldn't have been confused about what his grandma was saying, and I wouldn't have needed to call him over to translate for me.

It was when I realized that I needed to learn Spanish because I didn't want to be confused like that again. I started hanging out at that friend's house more often and gradually picked up on their language.

Until now, I can understand Spanish very well, although my accent is still funny according to that same friend, who I still hang out with a lot and go on hikes with monthly.

If you're in an area with people who speak a different language, it would be to your advantage to learn to speak their language.

That way you don't miss out on anything and also sometimes it's fun to listen to people talk when they think that you don't understand them.

Also, learning to speak a different language makes you smarter and helps you avoid little mishaps that happen because of things getting lost in translation.

Grammar

Grammar refers to the way your words are organized. You can be the most eloquent person out there knowing so many complicated words. You can also know every possible language out there. But, if your grammar is terrible, then your message won't be sent as clearly as you want it.

Now, most adults develop grammar naturally. The way most people normally speak in their native tongue is the correct grammar. The problem usually arises when you speak a different language.

For example, in English, you say, "I understand Japanese," but in Japanese, the grammar structure is "Watashi-wa Nihongo-ga Wakarimas" or in literal English, "I Japanese understand." If you're a native English speaker and you speak Japanese to a Japanese person, you might speak it in a way that follows the English grammar structure instead of their native grammar structure.

If you want to communicate effectively, you have to understand the grammar rules very well, and you have to structure your words and sentences in a way that doesn't muddle the message you're trying to relay.

Your Tone

Now that we're done with the actual words themselves let's go to the other stuff about the way you speak that gives context to what you're saying because really, there's a lot more to what you're saying aside from the words you use and one big part of it is the tone of your voice when you are speaking.

Here's how important your tone is. As an example, I want you to imagine the following:

1. Your mother yelling your first name.
2. Your lover gently speaking your first name.
3. Your friend casually calling you by the first name.

In each case, the same word is used, which is your first name. But, each is said in a different tone, and each case means a different thing than the others.

That's how effective tone is when you use it. The mere tone of your voice can be a message in itself. It indicates your mood and your intent.

Even if you use the nicest words you can find in your entire vocabulary and use the best, most eloquent grammar; it's still not going to come across as something good if your tone indicates hostility because you're yelling and the way you speak is pointed.

At the same time, even if you use the most hostile, offensive words you have and even threaten violence, the effect won't be as intimidating if you say it in monotone. I was actually going to say, "if you use a soft tone," but sometimes, violent threats can sound even scarier if spoken in a soft voice.

Your tone can easily change the context of your statements, so you have to understand how your tone of voice works and what the appropriate tone is for every message you want to send.

Your Speed

Aside from the tone of your voice, other indicators also exist, such as the speed of your speech.

Of course, there are times when you have to control the speed of your speech like when you're speaking to someone who is hard of hearing. In that case, you normally have to speak a little slower for the other person to be able to hear each word you are saying properly.

When you're in a hurry then, of course, you have to speak a little quicker than usual, so you can finish delivering the message in the short time you have to deliver it.

For the most part, however, when you don't consciously control the speed of your speech, it usually indicates your energy.

When you speak very fast, to the listener, it could indicate high energy. It's when you're excited or agitated. On the other hand, when you speak very slowly, then the listener might take it as a lack of enthusiasm on your part.

Sometimes, people even associate slow speech with a low level of intelligence because somehow, it seems like it takes someone who speaks slow, a little more time to process their own words.

So the speed you use when talking to people is also very important, and you need to be aware of it and control it as much as you can.

Your Volume

Your volume can say a lot, too, about the nature of the message you're trying to tell someone.

If you've ever whispered to someone's ear, then you know that you probably had to speak it softly to avoid being overheard by others. On the other hand, when you're watching a game, you're probably yelling loudly at the players because you want them to hear your frustration and tell them what they should be doing.

So basically, the volume of your voice could indicate how much you want to be heard.

I remember an uncle of mine who has hearing problems. He always yells his words because well, he can't hear himself speak, and he forgets that other people can hear fine, so when he can't hear himself, he thinks other people can't hear him as well.

So, he speaks loudly to hear himself speak and assure himself that the people he is speaking to can hear him as well.

Other than wanting to be heard, your volume can also indicate your confidence levels.

Usually, a shy person speaks softly because they're afraid of being heard and humiliated. On the other hand, a person who is self-assured may speak a little louder because they want to be clearly heard.

Nonverbal Communication

Now that you know the components of verbal communication and why each of them should matter to you, we'll discuss the components of nonverbal communication because communication is not just about what you are saying. It's also about what you are doing because everything you do sends a message, and as someone who wants to project charisma, you need to be aware of these as well and be able to master and control nonverbal communication as well.

Before we proceed to discuss the components of nonverbal communication, let me tell you the story of a man named Jeremiah Denton.

Back in the Vietnam war, he was captured and forced to go on a propaganda video in 1966.

While the video was being shot, he pretended to be irritated with the lighting used during filming and blinked while talking during the video. As it turned out, his blinking was a message in morse code saying "torture."

Since then, every video being sent out by kidnap victims, figures like terrorists and criminals, and politicians are thoroughly analyzed for hidden messages before anything else is done with them, like broadcasting on TV, for example.

Also, if you've ever seen the show Lie To Me, the premise is how they analyze nonverbal cues, which then becomes clues to solving crimes or resolving conflicts in the episodes. It's a TV show, but it doesn't mean that the concept of reading nonverbal cues is all fiction. It's actually being actively practiced.

As I said, your nonverbal cues also send a message, and you need to be a master of it as well and not just be reliant on verbal communication.

Proxemics

In simple terms, proxemics is the study of how you use space in social interactions. Basically, what it means is that the distance between you and another person and where you are relative to the things around you and the people you interact with have meanings.

I know it can still be a bit confusing, but I'm sure it will be a bit clearer once I go into further detail.

First, have you heard of the term "personal space?"

If you haven't or if you've heard it used but didn't fully understand what it means, then let me explain.

According to experts, particularly Edward T. Hall, in his book The Hidden Dimension, we have four different zones determined by our preferred distance when it comes to other people. I'm going to discuss it next, starting from the outer zone, down to the innermost zone.

First is the public zone, which is the outermost zone, and it's said to be between twelve to twenty-five feet or more.

In this zone, there's no physical or even eye contact. Think about when you shop at the department store. You try to keep a distance from the other shoppers as much as possible, right?

It's because you don't know them, and you're probably not even remotely interested in them.

The second zone is called the social zone, and it's anywhere from four to twelve feet away from you.

Again, think of shopping at the department store. Imagine meeting an acquaintance, maybe someone who you've seen at work a few times, and you want to say "Hi."

Or, maybe you saw someone you found interesting or is standing at a product you're curious about, and you want to ask for their opinion about the product. You get close to them, but not too close, right?

You just get close enough for them to hear you talk to them, but you keep a safe distance where they can't just reach you without you noticing or being able to react.

The third zone is called the personal zone, which is about eighteen inches to four feet from you.

This is the zone where you keep your friends and other people you're comfortable with, like certain family members. It's close enough to talk and to shake hands.

When you see a friend the department store, you approach them and even pat them in the back or shoulder for them to notice you if you were coming from behind.

The fourth zone is called the intimate zone, and it's from eighteen inches to direct contact.

It's usually where you keep the people you really care about and are really comfortable with, like your really close friends, significant other, or your children.

When you see them in the department store, you're comfortable enough to hug them or kiss them.

So, basically, the amount of distance you place between you and another person could be interpreted as your level of comfort and intimacy with them.

When you stand too far from a person, then they might take it as you not being comfortable around them.

In addition to the different zones, there's also your eye level in relation to another person, or how high you are positioned from the other person.

For example, you might get intimidated by someone who is far taller than you or when you're sitting, and they're standing in front of you while talking to you.

Usually, a higher position indicates power over the person in a lower position.

If you've seen the Star Wars prequels or at least have seen the meme where Obi-Wan Kenobi tells Anakin Skywalker that he has the higher ground and presumes that he has a greater advantage, it's like that.

That's why politicians and other people giving speeches are usually positioned higher using a stage or a podium. Someone giving a speech on a stage is going to be taken more seriously than someone who gives a speech on the ground floor. Of course, there are practicality issues that have to be considered, so it's not always true.

However, according to studies done in the medical field, in particular, doctor-patient relationships are significantly better when the doctor levels with the patient by stooping or sitting down than when they stand up and tower over a patient lying down in a hospital bed.

Gestures

Have you ever been in a conversation with a deaf or a mute person, or have you at least seen people use sign language?

Sign language itself is proof that gestures can be very powerful, sometimes even as powerful as words themselves when it comes to communication.

But, even if your speech or hearing is not impaired in any way, you still use gestures in regular everyday communication with other people.

Imagine that you're eating lunch at the office. You just took a big bite out of a turkey sandwich, and your mouth is full. Then, a coworker approaches you and asks you if the microwave is working, and you're really not sure. You can't talk with your mouth full, so how do you tell your coworker that you don't know?

Usually, you shrug. You raise your shoulders, tilt your head to the side, and if you can, you raise your hand, palm facing up. Without saying a word, you told the other person you don't know the answer to their question, and if they were paying attention, they would understand that you're telling them you don't know.

That's the power of gestures in communication. Now not all gestures are used in place of actual words. A lot of gestures are used together with spoken words and usually come out naturally without consciously controlling it.

For example, when you tell someone, "You, go over there!" Usually, you point at the person you're referring to then point at the place where you want them to go.

Another example is when you see people surrender in movies or shows, or even in the news. You'll see them put their palms up as if to show they have nothing in their hands.

If you want to be an excellent communicator, you have to understand gestures and be able to use them to send messages, as well as read them in order to get the correct message.

Posture

Your posture, or the way your body is positioned, also indicates a few things, including your mood, how you see the other person, and how you feel about the situation or interaction.

For example, what's called an open posture can project a sense of friendliness and positivity.

An open posture is when your feet are spread wide apart, and your palms face outward.

Think of when you're happy or in the mood to celebrate. Imagine winning the championship game of your favorite sport or winning a contest that you're really into. What's the winning position you take?

Are you familiar with the Jesus statue in Brazil? It's called the Cristo Redentor. Even if you're not a religious person, just look it up and imagine a person in that position looking at you. Normally, you would take it as a welcoming sign, right?

I mean, even with someone who is being aggressive saying "come at me bro!" would usually take that same position as if indicating that the violence is welcome.

If there's an open posture, there's also a closed posture. Examples are crossing your arms, having a clenched fist, or crossing your legs to your side away from the other person.

And of course, it sends the opposite message of an open posture. It indicates boredom or even outright hostility.

Think of bouncers at a club. What's their usual posture while standing by the entrance? The stereotypical club bouncer usually stands upright with arms crossed, right? They do it because they want to look tough, and it sends a message not to mess with them if you don't want to get hurt.

Touch

Touch is also one of those things that can deliver a message. For example, a handshake signifies agreement between two people.

When you close a deal with someone, you usually shake hands to close the deal, right?

Also, the way you touch someone can also send a message. Usually, a rubbing motion with your palm like how you would pet an animal can signify concern while a pat is usually a little more aggressive.

A soft touch can also indicate warmth, while a heavy hand can indicate aggression or frustration.

Of course, where you touch the other person also has a certain meaning depending on your relationship to the other person and how receptive they are, although it can be very controversial, so it's usually best to avoid touching someone you're not intimate with outside from a quick handshake.

Notes

Chapter 7.   Navigating Some Social Situations

W e've all been there. There's an event coming up, and either you *must* be there because of work, or family obligations, or because you simply promised you would and you don't want to come across like a person who doesn't keep their word, but you know it's going to be a rough time—potentially. Sometimes just the mixture of the crowd is a certain indication of troubled waters ahead, other times it's just one person who seems to spark unrest wherever he or she goes, but at the end of the day you just want to make it through the event with your dignity and confidence intact. So what can you do?

First of all, an important concept to begin to incorporate into your daily mindset is the fact that other people do not have control over us. While it's true that others *seem* to have the power to trigger certain reactions and emotions within us, the actual truth is that with enough practice, confidence, and presence of mind, *we* can be the ones in control of ourselves—and that includes emotional reactions.

You might ask, "How? How can I not react when somebody says something rude, hypercritical, or outrageous to me?"

To that we say: *practice,* and poise. Poise just isn't a word evoking some sort of Hollywood-esque facade, and it isn't about a proper-fitting suit or dress, or body posture. Poise is keeping your head under pressure. Poise is about inner strength in the face of adversity.

For starters, get cracking on your forgiveness potential. The biggest diffuser of negative energy should come as no surprise: forgiveness. When we forgive, we gain back our power. What happens when we *do not* forgive? a) we hold on to the negative emotion the other person sparked in us, be it hurt, anger, judgement, disgust, and b) we send that emotion back to the sender, and to anyone around us as collateral damage. Now we're spreading negative emotions like wildfire! That certainly won't earn us any charisma points, will it? (D&D references notwithstanding).

If instead, we stand in our power when the other person releases the offensive or triggering statement, and simply say, "That's all right", we've dispelled that negative energy. We're like a lightning rod channeling electricity's potential destruction safely into the ground, where it can be spread out and rendered harmless. Not only are we effecting ourselves with power and calm, but our response can be an example to anyone else around us, and perhaps encourage them to forgive (and then move on from) the offending speaker.

It's important to understand that other people may not possess the same skills, and if others *do* react negatively to the original offensive speaker, it's best to gracefully move on to more positive waters. At least we did not allow the negativity to directly effects us, and I would call that a win.

Other forgiveness phrases include:

- I understand.

- I hear you.

- Noted (in a positive voice, as this can also sound dismissive)

- We are all different, of course.

- You are absolutely entitled to your opinion.

- Thank you for sharing your point of view.

If the person questions your response, such as "Oh really?", simply return with "Yes." Then perhaps excuse yourself and move on to a different group of people, or wait for someone else to pick up the conversation.

There's an alternate set of responses in the case of someone saying something that you know is deeply offensive to one or more persons in the room. In the case of prejudice or hate, it's a rare individual who will not instantly feel a negative emotion in response.

~ 127 ~

At this point, your job is to refuse to add to the powder keg of the speaker's energy. Refuse to condone their words with a simple "I disagree", or "I would not share that here", and leave it at that. You may not be able to get this person to stop talking, but at least to those around you, you've quietly taken the side of being against hateful speech, while not contributing to the speaker's disruptive energy. Refuse to engage with them further.

Acceptance Gives You Freedom

Nobody in the world is perfect, which is good news, as it gives us freedom from believing that it's right to judge anyone else.

Learning to accept the fact that other people are different from ourselves is an important lesson, and it gives us great personal power when we achieve the acceptance state of mind. What's even more important is—extreme cases or instances aside—meeting and talking with someone who is vastly different from ourselves gives us a rare opportunity to expand our own understanding. When we set judgement aside and learn to accept people for who they are, we open our minds to new information and new context, that we can often use later on when faced with a challenge our own perspective is stumped by.

Never pass up an opportunity to learn. All of life is a journey of awareness and opportunity.

Learn to look at disagreements as misunderstandings.
When we remain in the pattern of "seemingly negative input =
emotional response", it can be incredibly difficult to move from
that point. We're stuck in a defensive position—where can we go
from here? No one will ever back down, give up, and say "I'm
sorry" simply because you think they're wrong, or that you are
offended by their words. In addition, none of that's the point—
we're not listening to the reasoning behind the words, we're not
considering what brought this person to this moment of belief. All
we hear is emotion, and that's what we're giving back. It's a
useless, endless cycle, and it lowers everyone involved instead of
showcasing their confidence and charisma.

If you take a moment and wait, center yourself and release that
negative emotion, you might then see the person in front of you—
unique, diverse, *different*, but also valid. Ask them to explain
what they mean. Look for points of similarity between yourself
and them. Offer up your own stories that might bridge the gap
between the two of you. You'll be surprised at how often a non-
negative reaction causes a conversation to become stronger, more
neutral, and in the end, rewarding.

Initiating A Difficult Conversation

Studies show that in the workplace, employees are forced to
navigate conflict related to managers or coworkers approximately
3 hours, at least, per week.

Obviously it isn't easy to do a great job if you're mired in emotion and negativity. What's even more disturbing is that the study also revealed that more than one third of these employees left their jobs rather than deal with the conflict at all. How can this problem be better handled, or even handled at all?

Most of instinctively know when we *should* have a difficult conversation with someone—be it at work, in the family, or with a friend or a partner. If you're already feeling the pull to the do the right thing, then you need to it, no questions asked. But how to rise to the occasion successfully? You'll need the two things you've been working on cultivating for greater charisma first: empathy and social skill. There's going to be a lot of navigation to reach a mutually agreeable destination. You'll also need courage, which as well know is not the *absence* of fear, but the acknowledgement of it, then the choice to move forward despite it.

Before you reach out to have the conversation, do some mental preparation in anticipation of it. Ask yourself "what could be the person's motivation for their behavior, and how is their behavior causing this problem?" Even more importantly, ask yourself "how is their behavior-driven problem affecting the (company, family, our relationship).

Get your thoughts on these two questions together, and take as much time as you need to have a central focus that you want to explore with the person, otherwise much of the initial conversation is simply going to be about discovery, and inevitably, defense.

You'll go off on far fewer tangents if you have a mental map of the road ahead before you reach out to the person.

Know what your objective is before you enter the conversation. You need to know what you want to accomplish before you start talking, otherwise the conversation is bound to become circular, and leave both parties hopelessly frustrated. Here's a checklist that can help organize your thoughts and goals:

- What is your best outcome to accomplish here?

- Is anything non-negotiable? Practice expressing this objectively.

- Plan on how you'll wrap up the conversation successfully.

- What action steps do you want to come out of this?

- What role do you want the other person to play regarding those action steps?

- Are you willing to support the other person after this conversation, and what support will you give, specifically?

Check your attitude at the door before the conversation begins.

You're not on a hunt and you're not here to target; you need to approach this conversation with an inquiry-based frame of mind. If you've already made up your mind about what's been going on and how to fix it, then you're not going to be successful here. Just as a physician should have a long, thorough talk with their patient before deciding on treatment, so should you listen to the other person's point of view and experience before reaching out to propose a compromise and solution to any problems that have been occurring. Even if you *think* you know exactly what the problem is, respect for the other person demands you listen to their thoughts. You may discover something you hadn't realized or thought about previously, and the impression you make by showing empathy and respect can go a long way into healing any fissures or divides that may have existed between you.

Emotions, however, are a different story. We can't properly utilize empathy if we strip all emotions from ourselves and omit them from the conversation. We can, however, refuse to follow a particular direction of what is called the "wheel of emotions".

In this particular emotional diagram, annoyance leads to anger which leads to rage, and so on. Knowing this, we can navigate the conversation back the other way. If emotions like shame, sadness, or regret lead to tears in the other person, we need to be strong enough not to judge them for that. Tears are *not* a sign of weakness, they're a sign of emotion, and we all have emotions so it's not our right to judge the next person for displaying them. Allowing the other person their emotional reactions puts us in a place of generosity and patience, and frames us in an empathic light.

If the other person does have a breakdown moment, we should acknowledge that this is perfectly okay, and allow them the time they need to collect themselves and return to the conversation.

If silence occurs, ride it out. Having difficult conversations is, well, *difficult*. We may need some time to collect our thoughts, and this is okay. Saying reassuring things like, "I can see how this could be difficult, and that's okay. Please take your time" can go a long way in making the other person feel respected and safe, and not pressured or put on the spot. Humans never react well when pushed into a position of defense, so make sure your body language and tone of voice don't contradict your words when you're trying to be reassuring.

Having high emotional intelligence, like charisma, is only partially inherent—most of it is learned.

You can prove that yours is high, right now, in the midst of this difficult conversation. Knowing that years of built up trust can be destroyed in mere moments makes it essential to preserve the relationship as you near the end of the conversation. No amount of acquiescence or promises is worth losing the relationship.

More time may be needed. Before you wrap things up, consider exploring how long changes could take to be initiated in the interest of both parties.

Don't be a hypocrite; preserve consistence. Never give one person a set of rules when another person doesn't have to follow that set of rules. If you think you're going to fool anyone, you're wrong—make sure that across the board, what applies to one applies to all.

Common Pitfalls We Might Encounter During a Difficult Conversation

Not everyone is going to be at their best when confronted in a difficult conversation, regardless of how objective, patient, and calm we are when approaching them. People sometimes adopt a defensive position because of their own fears and insecurities, and nothing we have said may be needed to trigger this. When people are in this position and trapped in a fear mentality, they may utilize something called a "thwarting ploy".

Pay attention to these and be ready to respond correctly if they occur:

- Stonewalling. This technique used by fearful and/or manipulative people involves putting up roadblocks to a conversation, such as questioning the validity of each thing the other person says, refusing to answer questions, and making generalized statements such as "this is ridiculous" or "I can't believe this is happening". **How to disarm this tactic:** For starters, always acknowledge a thwarting ploy. You can say here, "I won't be able to help if you keep putting up roadblocks, and I want this to be resolved in a way that puts you at ease. It will be easier for us to move forward if we stick to the topic. I appreciate your cooperation with this."

- Sarcasm. Another defense mechanism, and one that can be acknowledged by saying, "I know this is a difficult subject, which is why it's best if we both keep our tone neutral. "

- Being unresponsive. You can say, "I'm not sure how to interpret your silence. Take your time with this, but when you're able to express yourself, I am here to listen to you."

Pay Attention to Where You're Having the Conversation

The name of the game is *neutral territory*. If you're talking to an employee and you're a manager, your office is not the most suitable place. If you're an employee talking to your boss, ask if there's a more discreet place to talk, such as a conference room or lounge. If you're talking to a partner, friend, or family member, suggest a quiet public place such as a coffee shop.

This will help keep emotions under control as most people don't want to make a display in a public setting.

As for body language, remember to avoid the negative cues, such as arms crossed, tapping or fidgeting, and looking away from the person or staring for too long. If the person you're speaking to chooses to sit, you'll need to sit, also. If they prefer to stand, you've got a chance to avoid making them feel intimidating by sitting down.

Have an Idea of How to Start the Conversation?

Never *surprise* someone by initiating a conversation without warning. Give the other person a heads-up; reach out for a time and place to talk. Be specific about what you'll be talking about without labeling it or being accusatory, such as "Hey I wanted to meet up and talk about what happened the other day in the meeting. What time is good for you?" or "Let's take some time tomorrow to clear the air about some things. I'd like to hear your opinions about it. Why don't we grab coffee?"

Many of us put off these difficult conversations because we're at a loss as to how to initiate them, but with enough preparation and thought, we can get these much-needed conversations started, and hopefully discover some solutions that benefit everyone involved. Make sure your tone of voice carries no sound of judgement or accusal, but merely inquisitiveness and discovery.

What To Do If You're Approached For a Difficult Situation

Sometimes we find ourselves on the other side of the table. Perhaps we slipped up and reacted inappropriately to criticism, disrupting a meeting or group work effort. For starters, at this moment your charisma and reputation are at stake—this might make you want to revisit that discarded emotion of shame, but now is not the time for regression. Bite down and don't let shame overwhelm you—*everybody* makes mistakes. How one processes those mistakes separates the leaders from the led.

Give the person you're wishing to speak with time to process and prepare. In other words, never ambush someone—you will *never* get the results you want this way, unless the results you want are purely negative.

How to Approach Your Boss With a Concern

What happens if you have an issue and you're the one needing to ask for a meeting?

Don't act out of emotion. Wait until you've had time to cool down. If your first reaction is to go on the war-path, you are doing yourself a grave disservice. Take time to assess the situation and what you want to get out of a meeting your manager or boss.

Understand that the bigger picture is important to management.

A great manager will place themselves in an employees shoes for the purpose of empathy and understanding, but not every manager is a great one, and higher-ups are often overburdened by work load and lack of time. Therefore, even if your concern is strictly about you, such as a raise you thought you were entitled to, take time to frame your concern within the perspective of the work-group, branch, department, or company. If your raise was skipped this quarter, was that department-wide, and if so, is the company able to give a reason as to why the raises were delayed?

Speak logically, not emotionally. If you're angry that you didn't get a raise, that's valid, but don't frame your questions that way. Instead of saying "I'm furious that I've been skipped for a raise I was told was a sure thing", say instead "I'm sorry to have to talk about this with you, but my finances and budget didn't account for the lack of a raise I was assured was coming this quarter.

Can we talk about why that didn't happen, and what can I do to support you as you solve this issue?" Make it seem as if you and your boss are part of a team—chances are he or she has had to look at things that way many times, so this could be familiar, comfortable territory. On a daily basis you may never have to go beyond your own personal language and perspective to get your job done satisfactorily, but understand that managers are trained to think in a different vocabulary, and when we mimic that vocabulary we place them more at ease. Rise up to their level for the best results that will benefit *you*. Erase class and position barriers by proving you can utilize both empathy and reason.

Speaking Critically In a Public Forum

White House press members get rattled in such situations, so how are you supposed to handle a scenario where you pose critical questions or statements in a large company or town meeting? If it sounds daunting, it is, for everyone from the pros to the amateurs. You can take the edge off the situation with some preparation, however.

Avoid trigger, aka emotion-based language. Standing up and calling something "wrong" "stupid" "idiotic" or a "waste of time" is the wrong way to go; you're sure to never get to the end of a perfect storm of criticism and reaction. Give people a chance to actually *hear* what you're saying by stripping all emotion from it. Speak logically and calmly.

Know that even speaking this way, you will be met with criticism, potentially, and that criticism may not be constructive or objective. People most often respond with anger when it's a view they don't share. Promise yourself that you will retain your sense of poise and calm regardless.

Try to frame your statement in a way that acknowledges the majority.

"I realize that many or most of us think this (frame the subject), however, I want to shed light on a possible outcome that I think may not be in the best interest of the (town, community, organization, company)."

Don't stop, continue with proposed solutions you believe can help, then be prepared to really listen to what people are saying as they respond. Always reply to their responses and/or questions with a standard of *acknowledge what they said/propose alternative, or agree.*

If you keep your cool and remain centered, you may find more people coming over to your side and supporting your thinking on the matter.

How to Handle a Co-worker, Colleague or Peer Losing It

Here's where daily meditation comes in exceptionally handy. If you're side-swiped by another person's anger, *wait.*

Hold your action and steady yourself as you allow that person's emotions to travel through you and out, just like random thoughts did while you were meditating.

It's human nature to mirror the attack and respond in kind, but avoid this at all costs.

For starters, there's no need to apologize right away or at all, depending on the accusation or comment. The first thing you need to do is understand the basis of what they're talking about, and understanding requires calm questioning. If the other person is too tied up in their emotions to think straight, cut through the confusion with a quick, neutral observation: "Listen. I'm not going to trade insults with you—that won't solve anything. I'm ready to listen when you're calm enough to discuss this." Suggest you meet another time to try and work things out.

The other person may absolutely reject meeting another time, and so it will be upon you to move forward. Keep neutralizing the emotions with your responses. If the statements truly felt out of the blue and like an attack, you can admit that, "I don't know how to respond just yet. This is unexpected. What should our next step be?" This way you haven't yet conceded (because you don't know yet if you should, at least until you discover the details of what the other person is upset about), and you haven't tried to placate them.

If, however, you know you're in the wrong, own it, immediately. Apologize, and resist the urge to grovel. Ask what you can do to help if after the apology the person appears to calm down.

Whatever you do, don't sidestep or avoid conversations that need to happen. You're in training to be more charismatic and successful. Dodging difficult situations is not only counter-intuitive to that goal, but it causes you to miss important, intensive training opportunities that can greatly improve your skill level.

Notes

Chapter 8.   Ways of Improving your Charisma

There Are some people that seem to be naturally likable - it always looks like they were born likable. Well, this may be true, but you can also train yourself to become likable. No matter what your personality type is, you can always train yourself to exhibit some traits through constant practice. You can apply these traits to your character so that you can become more attractive, influential, and even trustworthy. Below are some basic tips for developing your charisma.

Start from Wearing a Warm Smile

A warm smile can never go wrong; it is a good point to start. With a smile, you will be able to set an emotional tone that will carry the audience with you on a journey. As you are speaking, you hope to get certain reactions of joy, suspense, anxiety, pride, concern, hope, or fear. You should be able to win all of these from your audience while you still appear to your audience like the Mr. Nice Guy.

Create an Emotional Connection with Your Audience When You Speak

Speaking is one of the earliest practices of humans. The earliest records of speech can be traced back to about fifty to a hundred thousand years ago. The oral tradition has made a lot of impacts on humans as it has molded all the societies of the earth over the years. This is certainly a lot of years for humans to be able to use this phenomenon to perfect their influence on other people and also situations.

Over the ages, there's been a lot of examples that one can reckon with when it comes to influential speaking. Abraham Lincoln, Winston Churchill, Martin Luther King, and the likes are some of these examples. These people were able to capture the attention of their audiences with every word that they spoke. What they had, which is the thing that made them stand out among their equals, was a very important life skill—charisma. When they spoke, it didn't matter who they were talking to or the number of their audience, they spoke in a way that their speech was felt by the members of the audience as though they were addressing each individual personally.

They all had styles that made them appear as though they didn't have to put in so much effort to deliver their thoughts in a well-fashioned manner. This is the technique that they used to captivate their audience.

Every time they moved as they spoke, their movements were in tune with the words they spoke, and they had an appearance that suited/appealed to the senses of their audience.

In line with the three elements of charisma, with effective practice and a lot of self-confidence, everyone will be able to gain charisma with this tip.

Also, what matters is the perception you have of your audience. The number of times that you have practiced before a mirror does not really matter; neither does the opinion of those around you about your message matters. Even though you may have an excellent speech to deliver, if you do not create an emotional connection with your audience, your message will not mean so much to your audience.

Typically, when people sit to listen to you, they do so with hopes that they are going to learn something new, so they listen with a sense of sympathy. What they want is to be inspired or to have a glimpse of your journey, so you have to make sure that you can give them what they want. What makes it easy is that they are open to bonding with you and building a relationship with you. This means that from the moment you start speaking, you have to set your mind at connecting with them.

Perfect the Mechanics of Speech

To be considered as one who speaks well, you have to space your words and your ideas. To do this, you have to be expressive with the tone which you deliver your speech with, and this should be at the right moments too. Try to breathe well and have enough energy to deliver your speech.

Make room for your listeners to pause when they should. This is very important for any speech. The best orators can space their speech in a way that allows the audience to be able to digest their ideas as they consider the next thing they are going to say. It is only very few people that can combine speaking and thinking. The power of your speech and what enables it to make the desired impact lies with the silences that come in the middle of your speech.

Tone also matters a lot in speech as it has some subtle effects that you may not easily take note of. If you are able to adopt the right tone and you can control your voice by chipping in the necessary emotional hints when they are appropriate, you will be able to control and make sure of the fact that your audience does not have doubts about the message you wish to pass across. When you maintain the right body language, your speech will naturally find the right tone.

As you talk, you are going to need a good amount of air to help you pass your message across. Can you recall the number of times you have witnessed people going off track on their speech when what they actually need to be doing is to be placing more emphasis on the theme of their message? It is very common for speakers to end their speech with the most important parts of their messages.

Ensure that you take in a good amount of air into your diaphragm such that you get the required energy that will help you deliver your last line with a 'blast.'

Your Body Should Match Your Words

Your audience will naturally feel uncomfortable if they notice that there is a disconnection between the things you are saying and the way you are saying them. When you are giving a positive message, for an instant, your body language should not in any way be defensive because it will arouse the suspicions of your audience as to whether you are being. Also, a positive message with a static body will also make the audience to feel you are not as excited about your message as you would want them to believe.

As you are speaking, you have to move at every point the language you use demands that you move. Make use of gestures and demonstrations when necessary to emphasize your words rather than trying to get attention from it.

Make use of facial expressions to give you hints about the way they are supposed to feel. With this, they will be able to flow with you at the same level.

Your Message Should Be Compelling

When you tell personal, authentic, and valid stories, your audience will be able to relate with you. This will bring you closer to them because, to them, you are no longer a distant voice from the podium. You may even become as close to them as a voice in their head or as a part of them, which they can always turn to; you become one that is sitting right next to them, who is sharing a special part of his/her journey with them.

There is a very special feeling that comes with a person confiding in another, and everyone can relate to that feeling. If an audience of different people and personalities are able to connect with you peculiarly, you would have won the crowd to yourself.

As you speak, your message has to assume a logical structure that is centered on a particular theme. It should be woven around a foundation that you are going to build upon as you proceed in the course of your speech. Your speech is best from a credible place that your audience is going to accept because they believe what you are saying. You must ensure that you don't make the deadly mistake of making your audience feel judged. Certainly, no one wants to face judgment day so early.

Practice Mirroring

If you wish to be charismatic at the moment, try to mirror your qualities. This entails that you try to adopt the qualities of someone else (someone you admire or whom you consider to be a charismatic person). Try to match up with his gestures, mannerisms, and his energy. By doing this, you are going to notice that people will respond to the attributed you have mirrored just as they would with the person whose attributes you are adopting. This does not mean that you are going to agree with all the things they do or everything they say. The only thing you are imitating to a reasonable extent, the way they act. This may come quite naturally for you, but it depends largely on your social setting. However, it is a simple way of boosting your likeability.

In doing this, you have to select those qualities that you consider to be likable to other people. Observation is a very important factor in your journey to improving your charisma. As Joyce Newman, the head of the Newman Group, says, you have to look up to those people whom you consider as charismatic. According to him, you don't have to imitate them; what you need to do is to learn their secrets, then apply them to yourself. You should polish them until they suit you perfectly. Note that this is a process of trial and error.

Take Hollywood or any other industry, for example, and you will notice that there are charismatic people everywhere.

Note the way the best actors in these industries carry themselves. Use them as your yardstick by picking their most effective and charismatic qualities for your use. By emulating those people whom you think are likable, you will be able to learn some things about how you can also become likable.

Have Fun

People make the mistake of associating public speaking with a feeling of horror, inconvenience, freight, anxiety, or even torture as if the entire process or experience is a scene from a nightmare. It does not have to be like this when you speak (to a large or small audience), you should do it as though you are also a member of the audience. Think of the things you like to see in your speaker; do you want them to carry on in a stiff manner, or you prefer to see them enjoying his or her experience? I guess a lively speaker will appeal more to you.

By enjoying your presentation or speech, you give the impression that you were not forced to do what you are doing because you like that you are doing it, and not that you are doing a lot of hard work and are passing through a lot of stress.

Your audience will not only see you as one who has something important to say, but they will be grateful for the fact that they did not miss the chance to listen to you. The mere fact that you enjoy talking to them will make them feel like you have something 'cool' to give them, and it is just a matter of time before they too will begin to enjoy themselves.

Put a Lot of Energy in Your Voice

When you talk, you should be as audible as possible. Have you ever listened to someone whom you strained your ears to hear? Soft-talkers and presenters who lack energy are the types that stress their audience by making them strain their ears to listen to them. These speakers seem so far away from their audience as they make them (the audience) feel like they are being left out of the message they are meant to get.

When you speak, you should ensure that it is able to gather a lot of vocal power to enable you to get to everyone that is listening to you. This should include those that are seated at the back who would ordinarily not find it easy to hear you. Keep in mind that your vocal energy varies in different scenarios as it will need to be high with a large audience and in an open space. When you are using a mic, also, you should ensure that you tone your voice down. If you notice that where you are speaking in is echoing, you should try to speak slowly so that you will not end up overriding your speech.

By projecting the necessary amount of energy during a presentation, everything will be made easy for those who are listening to you. They will feel relaxed instead of stressing to help you do a part of your job.

Notes

Chapter 9.   Using the Power Words to Increase Your Magnetism, Tactics to Increase Your Charisma and Transform into a Social Magnet

Charisma

M ost of us think charisma to be a rare quality that is bestowed to a few lucky souls. Others believe that it belongs to some special people who end up being highly visible and get rewarded for high positions in the political world. In other words, charisma is something that can be learned as it has everything to do with the mindset of persons as well as their nonverbal behaviors that are associated with it. Charisma at times seems like a superficial quality at a glance. However, if you are keen in observing its traits, you will understand that it is a combination of power, warmth, and presence. Through that, one can easily connect with people around their vicinity with ease. Therefore, charisma is for anyone who has a strong desire for increasing their magnetism as well as opportunities of increasing their success.

It belongs to those who want to have a more meaningful and engaging character in life by positively impacting the lives of others.

Take a look at some of the key ideas that can help shy people to become more engaged as public speakers even in areas they thought they would not make.

Presence

It is worth noting that even toddlers have charisma. The kids are wide-eyed and curious. Hence, they can capture the attention of a room full of adults without even saying a word. Do you remember any time when some of these toddlers caught our attention? You might be wondering why yet they did not say even a word. Maybe because they are cute or something. However, a lot has to do with their presence. During such situations, toddlers are entirely in that moment, and some magnetism gives the people around them 100 percent of their attention. Think of someone like Michael Jordan. When he was playing for the Chicago Bulls in the early 1990s, the team won two consecutive NBA cups. His focus on each game made a difference such that he became so contagious among his teammates. His teammates also elevated their game, and in the long run, they emerged as winners. Everyone wanted the bulls to win.

The aspect explains why his line of clothing sells well for Nike even after twenty years down the line. Jordan isn't different from the toddler. His presence is what makes all the difference.

In other words, we can say that if someone like Jordan is in the moment, he is probably thinking about nothing else. It is worth noting that adults are in most cases in a state of partial continuous attention. Most people are not fully engaged with their employees or co-workers, their spouses, even their children let alone the grocery clerks. In other words, people have divided attention to all the parties that affect their lives. The aspect causes them not to be charismatic as they would wish. The result is shyness that tends to rob off our abilities. It is worth noting that for one to master the First, part of charisma, the substantial presence of someone means a lot.

Many ways can help you become more engaged and overcome the feeling of being shy. One you need to focus on your breathing. You need First, to fill your lungs with air and then attend to your senses as you breathe out. The other practical way of becoming more present is by maintaining eye contact with those you are speaking to. You don't have to give them a hard stare, wear a smile, and engage them in all of your conversations. Be warm and friendly as you talk to them. The aspect will attract more attention, and people will be willing to listen to you speak. Some will fall in life with your voice and maybe starts imitating you.

The aspect allows you to understand that you are imparting something in their lives as well.

The body language we use when communicating reveals an apparent lack of interest. For instance, if you are speaking to the public and your shoulder is turned away, it might indicate that you are shy or you are not interested in what you are trying to explore. Also, if you are easily distracted by texts, it shows that you are not at the moment. The aspect reveals to the audience, and they may not be interested in listening to what you are trying to communicate. Thus, you need to square up your body and the shoulders as well. Try and look directly at those you are conversing with and maintain that eye contact. You may not be able to bake to be at the moment always, but when you have time, make use of it and explore all the lope holes that might indicate that you are shy.

Power

It is worth noting that power is defined in different ways. However, when it comes to charisma, authority refers to a perception by others that have influenced and agency and makes things happen. In most cases, people are assigned power automatically due to their wealth, the position of authority, or even physique. However, you don't have to possess all these aspects to be convincing.

The perception of influence and agency is determined in a large percentage by the body language as well as the non-verbal cues one uses. Aspects such as postures, dress as well the voice that one uses determines the level of attention that one draws for the public. It is good to widen your stance and open your arms, not like a super-hero but to a comfortable position. If you are speaking to an audience while sitting, sit in an upright position. It is also good to know when to listen and when to speak. Dominating a conversation at times doesn't make a person be more powerful.

In most cases, it may have an opposite effect when people realize that the discussion is taking one side. It is essential to nod your head selectively. At times one needs to at listening rather than constantly nodding to every idea that comes across. The other aspect that puts people off is pitching one`s voice at the end of every sentence rather than increasing it. As you communicate, think of cues that will increase your perception of personal power. It is critical to understand that charisma becomes stronger when the presence, as well as power, are combined with genuine warmth. The aspect creates a stronger bond between the speaker and the audience. The conversation becomes livelier, and one gets more attached to it. It increases the presence of an individual done in the long run the power within the person is defined as charisma.

Warmth

If you have power, you pose the perception that you can make things happen. However, if you have kindness, you represent the knowledge that you will use the control you have for the good of others. It is worth noting that warmth is similar to the present, you can`t fake it. In other words, you can Smile and have polite manners as you speak, but you, can`t you can create a warm atmosphere. The aspect is linked to the fact that warmth comes from a more profound meaning rather than being a peasant. In other words, you can quickly tell or notice the presence of someone who has genuine affection for us. Thus, since one can`t fake presence or warmth, it is essential to remove all the barriers that hinder the natural heat for others.

In most cases, the most significant barrier that people have with creating warmth is the attitude that people have on certain aspects. In most cases, negative minds rob off the heat may create. However, you need to develop affection with your public and envision yourself as the audience. Feeing their kindness and accepting their aspect and feel them. Consider the elements of charisma that you possess and explore your weaknesses. The elcment will increase your power and presence in the conversation.

Disciplined

Even if you are shy, you need to be disciplined. You need to train yourself on the need to be focused, especially when other people are speaking. You need not be glancing at others or thinking about your busy schedule and answering messages while someone is talking to you. In the same way, there is no way you can be speaking to an audience, and you need to be disciplined. There is no way you will keep talking with your phone and expect your audience to listen to you. Most of them will be distracted by your attitudes as well as the behaviors you possess in public. Also, being charismatic doesn't necessarily mean that you must speak. There are times that you ought to listen. In other words, charismatic people often make the speaker feel as if he or she is the only one in the room. They will do everything to ensure that they capture the attention of the speaker. The aspects pave the way for more acceptances, and the other audience may even elect him or her for the representative position. For instance, if a political leader is speaking to a particular group of people, a charismatic person among the audience will ensure that the leader notices their efforts in capturing what they are trying to speak. In the long run, the other viewer agrees with him or her, and they might receive a representative position. The aspect is drawn by their attention as well as the presence they bring from the conversation.

Convey the Right Message

The best thing about involving a person in the conversation is by mirroring the body language that fits what they are speaking about. At times, it is advisable to avid speech patterns such as, uh, or you know. They piss someone offs, and one may feel uncomfortable speaking to you. If it comes to agreeing, nod your head systemically. Add phrases as I agree with you at times. It is not advisable to keep nodding your head even in places where the speaker or the audience wants you to alter a word. Always be prepared to learn. Also, if you are the main speaker of the event, being shy doesn't mean that you don't have a chance of learning. Learn to take a positive mindset for whatever is coming up. There are cases where the audience tends to be violent or disagree with your statements. You didn't have to sink to stop speaking. Listen to them and allow them to take the day as you get composed. The aspect will enable them to re-accept you and offer their hatred for you to keep speaking. However, if they disagree or boos, and you try silencing them by pitching up your voice, you may end up harming yourself as well as others who might be willing to listen to you. It is worth noting that you can't create warmth for everyone in any audience. Other people will see the negativity on you. Thus, if they boo and you are keen to sense them, they may heighten their arguments, and you may end up losing heart.

Be Aware of Feelings

Even if you are shy, you need to be charismatic via the few words you may be able to speak. However, you need to be very careful with how you treat the feelings of individuals. You need to acknowledge the presence of other individuals and try to understand what they are feeling. For instance, if someone appreciates you as you speak, you may need to pause and say a sincere thank you. It is important to look directly at the persons and let them understand that you appreciate their efforts. The aspects give them more courage and confidence to complement you later. It will also attract the attention of others who might be seeing their negativity in your speech. You also need to develop some power of persuasion. In other words, you need to possess some abilities you can use to motivate others to follow you. You might be having terrific ideas, but the way you persuade others determines whether they will follow you. You need to learn about some of the obstacles that may hinder your audience from understanding some of your non-verbal cues. At times, it is advisable to use human touch to personalize a conversation rather than rushing over it. For instance, patting someone on their back or touching their elbows while making a point may attract the attention of the person you are speaking to rather than assuming their feelings.

It is worth noting that just like presence and warmth, you can't fake charisma. It is an attitude or behavior that you develop with time. Even if you are shy, you can learn how to be more charismatic and overcome all your fears. However, all the steps, as well as the attributes behind being charismatic need one to work hard and be committed, let alone being patient. A bodybuilder uses her time and resources to do some weight lifting here and there and eventually achieves his or her desires. In the same way, you need to develop some attractions that will increase your charismatic nature. Learn some of the few words that attract the attention of your audience quickly.

Creativity is the key to succeed in everything. It is worth noting that every speaker wishes to attract the attention of his audience and communicate his or her ideas. However, what brings a difference is the aspect of creativity. You need to develop some sense of ownership to whatever you are speaking. The element will allow you to make some sentimental decisions that will ensure that your presentation is perfect. You may be presenting a similar piece with someone else. However, what makes the difference is the way you use some of the non-verbal and increase your presence. For instance, all of us are speakers in one way or another. But there are good speakers than others. There are also good and bad teachers. But what makes a difference is the presentation of ideas.

Even if you are shy, you need to develop some of these aspects that cause one to be charismatic. You might be having a few words or short speeches to present due to your shyness nature. But that should not deter you from being charismatic.

You need to be creative and make the best of the time you are given. Don't do the obvious, but try and add some uniqueness to attract the attention of your audience. If you are among the audience, be an active listener, and communicate the right message. Encourage the speaker by either agreeing with what they are trying to communicate. You should never underestimate any one's feelings. However, leaner to appreciate the efforts of each person. You don't have to be dominant or wealthy to be charismatic. However, you need to be productive with ideas and personalize your conversation to win the confidence of your audience as well.

Notes

Conclusion

Charismatic people draw others to them because they make others feel good about themselves. This is a skill which can be learnt and improved upon daily. If you are not confident trying all the techniques described in this book then it is advisable to start small. Set yourself a goal of achieving just five of them within the next week, practice on those closest to you and watch your charisma grow.

Within a few weeks you will be using all the techniques described and the effects will be noticeable. As your charisma grows you will feel more confident and more able to deal with any situation; this will improve your appeal to others and create an ever increasing spiral which builds your personality. You will no longer be the person on the sidelines trying to fit in; you will not even pause to entertain negative thoughts. These simple techniques can be used by anyone and will ensure you become the person you both want to be and can be. Others will look to you for inspiration and advice; in fact, you will be the one that others refer to when they say I wish I had the charisma you have.

As you put these principles into practice it will become second nature to you and this is the time when you should ensure you stay grounded. Different techniques work for different people; ten minutes meditating in the morning or breathing exercises can help. Some people prefer to have a poignant note or reminder on their fridge door; the method will be unique to you but the result must be to keep you grounded. The moment you think everyone gyrates towards you because you are so important is the point at which you will switch from charismatic to arrogant; this is not a feature anyone finds attractive.

Everything takes time. Learning takes time. Building your charisma takes time. You have to just keep pushing and applying everything you've learned to the best of your abilities. Even people born with natural charisma don't always end up being able to fully utilize it unless they keep using it and polishing it over the course of their lives, so don't be frustrated if you don't see immediate results.

Just keep pushing, learning, building your confidence and communication skills, and of course, your overall charisma. If you do that, then you'll get there before you even realize it. Remember, charisma can be learned and developed. Sure, some people have a natural talent for charisma, but even those born with it don't always develop it. But you, you're different. You are going to build your charisma, and you are going to keep pushing until you get to where you've always wanted to be.

Charisma is not a gift that some people have and others do not, it is a skill which needs to be learnt and can make a huge difference to your life. In essence it is a way of building confidence in your own abilities and being ready to undertake any situation; no matter what happens. You should never be afraid to try something new or enter a new situation; it may lead to bigger things or it can simply be chalked up to experience. You are more likely to regret the things you have not tried than the things you did, even if they were failures. Build your charisma with these techniques and live the life you want!

CPSIA information can be obtained
at www.ICGtesting.com
Printed in the USA
BVHW011212040321
601707BV00001B/3

9 781914 395642